PRAISE FOR *THE ALIG*

C000142855

"Richard Nugent has ripped up the rulebook, dispelled the myths and shared his winning formula of what it takes to be truly successful. This is the book that will make your business better."
Michael Heppell, keynote speaker and author

"A practical set of tools that anyone can use from a departmental level, divisional level and all the way up to corporate. A strategic gamechanger for consumer-facing industries."
George Paige, Global Head of Brand and Creative, Etihad Airways

"A brilliant resource, punctuated with insightful interviews. This book is full of immediately actionable ideas all contained within a practical framework."
Davey Barrett, Director of Creative and Intellectual Property, Mattel Adventure Park

The Alignment Advantage

*Transform your strategy, culture
and customers to succeed*

Richard Nugent

KoganPage

First published in Great Britain and the United States in 2023 by Kogan Page Limited

2nd Floor, 45 Gee Street
London
EC1V 3RS
United Kingdom
www.koganpage.com

8 W 38th Street, Suite 902
New York, NY 10018
USA

4737/23 Ansari Road
Daryaganj
New Delhi 110002
India

© Richard Nugent 2023

ISBNs
Hardback   9781398610637
Paperback   9781398610606
Ebook   9781398610620

British Library Cataloguing-in-Publication Data
A CIP record for this book is available from the British Library.

Library of Congress Cataloging-in-Publication Data
Names: Nugent, Richard, author.
Title: The alignment advantage : transform your strategy, culture and customers to succeed / Richard Nugent.
Description: London ; New York, NY : Kogan Page, 2023. | Includes index. |
 Summary: "Strategy, culture and customers are the key elements of any business. But to truly succeed, they need to be effectively built, refined and aligned. Studies show that organizations which are highly aligned are 72% more profitable than their competition. The Alignment Advantage shows how you can achieve this through a practical and proven framework which can be adapted to all businesses, whether it's a small start-up, multinational organization or somewhere in between. Arguing that Peter Drucker's claim that "culture eats strategy for breakfast" is counterproductive and Simon Sinek's "start with why" approach is compelling yet flawed, Richard Nugent dismisses flawed approaches and creates a clear, accessible blueprint for a more collaborative, data-driven and efficient organization. Illustrated with fascinating case studies from the likes of LEGO and Nike, The Alignment Advantage cuts through organizational silos and inter-departmental tensions to provide an aligned and strategic approach that will allow you to build your success, refine your processes and align your efforts to target your customers and clients"-- Provided by publisher.
Identifiers: LCCN 2023012132 (print) | LCCN 2023012133 (ebook) | ISBN 9781398610606 (paperback) | ISBN 9781398610637 (hardback) | ISBN 9781398610620 (ebook)
Subjects: LCSH: Strategic planning. | Corporate culture. | Organizational effectiveness. | BISAC: BUSINESS & ECONOMICS / Strategic Planning | BUSINESS & ECONOMICS / Organizational Development
Classification: LCC HD30.28 .N839 2023 (print) | LCC HD30.28 (ebook) | DDC 658.4/012--dc23/eng/20230317
LC record available at https://lccn.loc.gov/2023012132
LC ebook record available at https://lccn.loc.gov/2023012133

Typeset by Hong Kong FIVE Workshop, Hong Kong
Print production managed by Jellyfish
Printed and bound by CPI Group (UK) Ltd, Croydon CR0 4YY

Kogan Page books are printed on paper from sustainable forests.

This book is dedicated to every business owner who faces into the unknown every day.

And every leader who strives to make the lives of their people better, while trying to deliver what needs to be delivered.

Most of all it is written with thanks to Joanne, Sam, Will and George, for your patience, support, love, laughter and lessons in life.

CONTENTS

Introduction 1

What is the 5% Club? 2

How to make the most of this book 4

01 Busting business myths 5

Myth 1: Culture eats strategy for breakfast 5

Myth 2: Great organizations start with why 7

References 12

02 The three key components of the ALIGNED® framework 13

Strategy 13

Culture 14

The X 15

More terms to be aligned on 16

Reference 26

03 How to gain the Alignment Advantage 27

Six questions to start the Alignment Advantage 27

Strategy and culture 29

Culture and the X 30

Culture is the pivot in the Alignment Advantage 30

04 The strategic starting point 39

Defining your key strategic objective 40

More examples of key strategic objectives 43

Summary 45

05 How to build an ALIGNED® strategy 49

Strategic fog 51
Strategic alignment 53
Breaking down the key strategic objective into enabling
    objectives 55
Continuing the strategic alignment process 56
Is your organization too fast-paced to have a proper
    strategy? 57

06 The truths and half-truths about culture 59

Creating a purpose, values and vision does not create a
    culture 60
Big bang launches don't work 60
The brand values conflict 61
A good culture is a nice culture 61
Purpose and values – the distinctions 62
References 71

07 Crossing the cultural chasms 73

Crossing the chasm 73
The business case for cultural change 74
Define your cultural landing point 75
Create a clear, shared cultural narrative 78
The curse of underestimating scale 78
Ensure the leadership team are fully committed and aligned 79
Create a strategy to bring the culture to life 81
Engaging the masses 81
The magic 20 per cent 82
Develop and mobilize cross-level, cross-discipline change
    teams 87
Initiate multiple business projects with slightly unrealistic
    timescales 89
Getting to the cultural landing point 93
Maintaining cultural consistency 95
Reference 96

08 ALIGNED® performance management 97

Performance measures 97
Bringing ALIGNED® performance measurement together 100

09 What is the X and why? 109

More on the service/experience distinction 110
Three drivers of loyalty 113
Measuring guest experience 117
A word on NPS 118
Outcomes are the foundation of ALIGNED® measurement 120
The true meaning of brand 123

10 ALIGNED® teams 131

Is this a team or a work group? 132
Can you afford to tolerate brilliant jerks? 133
Does your team take joint and several responsibility? 134
What is most important – a high-performance team or a high-
    performing team? 135
Do you trust each other enough to have the right degree of
    conflict? 137

11 ALIGNED® communication 145

Outcome-driven 146
State-driven 147
Experience-driven 148

12 Living an aligned life 161

Your life strategy 162
How do you want your life to be? 163
Your life's X 164
Align your life 165

Index 175

Introduction

Becoming part of the 5% Club

Over the past twenty years, I have worked with some of the best and most well-known organizations in the world. I have learned from and studied with some of the most brilliant people in the fields of leadership, culture, personal development and change. In many ways, this book is a culmination of this journey.

However, it would be misleading to say that the alignment advantage was born from a desire to create a product. Instead, the methodology and its results were, initially at least, emergent. The advantages that come from aligned understandings of strategy, culture, brand and customer experience were obvious to see in those select few organizations that focused on that alignment. The negative impact caused by a lack of alignment, and the challenges caused by myths around strategy and culture, were equally stark. It became impossible to ignore the Alignment Advantage, and over the past four years the methodology has stood up to test after test. It is as robust as it is powerful. For most organizations and teams, the ALIGNED® methodology will not just create a huge advantage, it will also be revolutionary.

By reading this book and applying your learning and insights, you will break down silos in your organization. You will unite teams. You will refine what needs to be delivered and the systems, processes and structures to achieve what needs to be achieved.

You will make your organization a better place to work – at least for those who really want to contribute to its success. Vitally, you will create clarity about what your customers should experience.

On a personal level you will have a greater understanding of strategy, and how to create and execute it, than most other people in your organization. You will have a clearer understanding of what really drives organizational culture. You will have a framework for changing culture, and you will be able to use your understanding to build teams and organizations that feel connected and collaborative.

You will be able to see through some of the common myths about brand and customer experience in a way that many in organizations of all sizes can't. If you are in a position to make the changes necessary, your customers, clients and guests will notice the difference. They will feel differently about your product or service, and you will have the tools to measure their new experience.

By making the most of the Alignment Advantage, you will become part of the 5% Club.

It is worth acknowledging that if you are a leader who is committed to their business, you will read the first couple of chapters of this book and assume that you, your team and your organization are already part of the 5% Club; however, the chances are that you aren't. It is much more likely that you are among the 95 per cent that aren't aligned.

That isn't a criticism; instead, you are about to uncover an amazing opportunity.

What is the 5% Club?

Over the past five years we have worked with hundreds of teams, groups and organizations, and assessed them to discover how aligned they are strategically, culturally and in the experiences that they want to create for their customers, clients, guests or visitors.

The results of our diagnostics are consistently stark. Fewer than 5 per cent of the most senior teams in organizations of all sizes are clear and aligned in their understanding of strategy, culture and customer experience. More importantly, and surprisingly to our clients, in 95 per cent of cases those teams are not aligned on what the key strategic objectives they are working to deliver are, whether their culture is right for what they are being entrusted to deliver, and on the experience they are trying to create for their customers. In short, most executive teams think that they are aligned, yet they aren't.

Those who *are* fully aligned take a competitive advantage in their sectors that looks almost inexplicable to those who aren't looking through an ALIGNED® lens. Take the UK retailer Sports Direct as an amazing example. The company was founded in 1982, and at the time of writing is the UK's largest sporting goods retailer. In 2021 the Sports Direct division of the Fraser Group's reported revenue was in the region of £1.4 billion. However, this success is not without criticism or controversy.

If I were to ask a group of 100 people at a conference whether they had ever shopped at Sports Direct, around 80 per cent would put their hands up. If I asked that 80 per cent what Sports Direct's strategic intent is, the answer is unequivocal – stack it high, sell it cheap.

If I ask that same group about the organization's culture, the answers are as consistent. The vast majority of people say that they would not want a family member to work there. There is a strong perception that its young frontline workforce is not too well taken care of.

As for our experience as customers, most of us expect long queues, and frenetic staff who do their best to get what their customers want in a reasonable timeframe. The expectation of what we would call the X are low. Yet, despite all of Sports Direct's many perceived faults, so many of us go back time and time again. We contribute to one of the most astounding success stories in the UK retail sector in recent history.

Why is Sports Direct such a success? One key factor is, undoubtedly, the fact that they are a shining example of the Alignment Advantage in full effect. Their strategy is crystal clear for all to see and understand. Their culture is perpetuated and is exactly what is needed to deliver their strategy. And everything about their brand and customer experience is aligned perfectly with their culture and strategy.

While Sports Direct isn't necessarily the coolest organization, it is a perfect example of one that has grabbed a huge competitive advantage by aligning their strategy, culture and expected customer experience.

How to make the most of this book

I have written this book to be used in two ways. Firstly, use the book to develop your understanding and clarity of the three main components of the ALIGNED® framework. You will also have a deeper and clearer understanding of how these elements must interact with each other. I would love you to share your new found understandings with your colleagues and team members. The insights alone will build even greater success for you all.

Secondly, I would like you to use the book as a toolkit. It should prompt action. While I want you to enjoy the book, it is much more important that it creates new ways of thinking and operating. In short, read and do, read and do, read and do.

The methodology around which this whole book has been created will allow you to position yourself as an expert, and to lead your people and your business better. You will get better results, bring teams together, and make decision-making better and easier. Please make the most of the competitive advantage you have in your hands right now.

01

Busting business myths

One of the greatest pleasures of developing the ALIGNED® methodology was challenging some longstanding and unhelpful business myths. I have studied leadership and worked with organizations for twenty years, and I have seen and heard so many unhelpful half-truths take root, cause conflict and inefficiency, and cause leaders to challenge what they know to be inherently right.

In this chapter I lay two of these myths bare. If my challenges feel uncomfortable to you, I urge you to involve others in your organization in the conversations about the myths. It may be that the approaches have served you at some point, but do they serve you now? As our organizations reshape themselves after a global pandemic and look to take advantage of the possibilities of hybrid working, it is vital that we challenge these two myths that hold us back from the advantages brought about by strategic and cultural alignment.

Myth 1: Culture eats strategy for breakfast

This myth is built on a quote attributed to the world-famous author, educator and consultant Peter Drucker. By the time Drucker died in 2005, aged 95, the Australian had authored 39 books which shaped many facets of modern thinking about organizations and how they should be managed and led.

To say that I respect Peter Drucker and his work is a considerable understatement. I believe that he was almost unfathomably ahead of his time in his thinking about how to connect human performance to organizational success. It is no wonder then that hundreds of quotes attributed to him are still prominent and influential in the business world today.

The proposition is that culture is more important than strategy and so that is where you should focus your efforts. Throughout this book I, and those that I interview, will show why this isn't true. So given the reverence that I have for Drucker and my complete disagreement with the notion that culture should be set up as being superior to strategy (or vice versa, but I will come to that in the next chapter), you can imagine my delight when I discovered that Drucker never actually said that 'culture eats strategy for breakfast'. In fact, the first citation of Drucker saying it appeared in 2011, six years after his death.

The fact that the quote is misattributed is, of course, not my biggest problem with it. Nor is it its metaphorical ambiguity.

My main issue is that it invents a conflict between two vital components of a successful organization. It reinforces misunderstandings about the 'hard' strategy and the 'soft' culture, and it sets up a more and a less important side of the partnership. This kind of thinking helps to divide senior teams, creates silos and causes organizational conflict.

Instead of thinking of strategy and culture as combatants in a war of importance, we must instead think of them as partners in organizational success.

You must shape your organization's culture to be an enabler of your strategy. I will continue to reinforce this message throughout this book. If you don't align your culture to your strategy, it will, more than likely, become a strategic blocker. However, to do this, the leaders in the organization must be clear and aligned as to what the strategy is. Culture can't enable strategy unless the strategy is clear.

Another way to think about this is that strategy and culture are two cogs that drive each other. They work together to enable organizational achievement. When they are misaligned, the organization cannot perform at its best.

Culture does not eat strategy for breakfast. If I were to extend the metaphor I would be much more likely to say that they are two of the three ingredients required for a healthy and nutritious meal that will set you up for a successful day.

Myth 2: Great organizations start with why

This is perhaps an even more challenging myth for me to debunk. For many years, Simon Sinek's legendary 2009 TED Talk 'How great leaders inspire action' was a formative part of my leadership thinking. It has been watched over sixty million times (Sinek, 2010).

In case you haven't seen it, the presupposition is that the difference between great organizations like Apple and the rest is that this organization started with a purpose or core belief. This helped Apple to engage people in a way that others couldn't. It is a compelling proposition that lands well for reasons I will come onto very soon.

I love Sinek's early work. I love his model, the Golden Circle, and I love how he articulates it. However, there is one fundamental challenge. The notion that great organizations start with why (purpose) rather than what (strategic intent) simply isn't true.

Let's take Apple as the primary example, as it is central to Sinek's TED Talk. He outlines beautifully that Apple was built on a core belief of 'everything we do, we believe in challenging the status quo, we believe in thinking differently'. Sinek then moved on to describe how this translates into action – 'the way we challenge the status quo is by making our products beautifully designed, simple to use and user friendly. We just happen to make great computers'.

It is a compelling case and can be useful from a cultural or brand perspective. Still, it isn't accurate to say that this is the foundation of Apple as an organization.

When Steve Jobs and Steve Wozniak started the business, they produced circuit boards with a computer processing unit and a memory board. These products that would evolve to change the technological landscape did not yet have their own keyboards, but the creators and a multimillionaire investor, Mike Markkula, saw a commercial opportunity and maximized it.

In short, Apple started as a company that made and sold computers to make money.

This is a strategic decision. In Sinek's terms, they started with a what, not a why. The why came much later.

Even in the subsequent phases of Apple's growth and evolution, its success was based on strategic and technological development such as its cell-based colour graphics, open architecture and its selection as the platform for the business application VisiCalc.

Purpose (why) has become a central conversation in the formation of so many organizations, but sadly, I believe, to the detriment of good, solid strategic thinking. Before we get to the 'why' we must give at least some thought to the what. Even my own organization started with a clear decision about what type of organization it would be (a consultancy), what kind of work we would do (leadership development) and what income it must generate to make it viable for my family and me. I also made some clear decisions about the structure of the business. While it was a far cry from a detailed strategy, it created the strategic foundations upon which I am proud to have built a successful business that has partnered with brilliant clients in every continent of the world.

And yes, we have a core belief, but that came later in the development of the business.

Central to the Alignment Advantage is the understanding that we must shape our organization's culture to be a strategic enabler. By nature then, we must be crystal clear on what our strategy is, and, in Sinek's terminology, strategy is our 'what'. While he makes a wonderfully compelling case for the idea that great organizations start with why, unfortunately it is a brilliant business myth.

The lesson from both these myths is that it can be easy to be swept along by a great message, especially when it is delivered well. However, to paraphrase the pioneer of accelerated learning, Dave Meier (Meier, 2000), we must all approach business buzzwords and models like a bird approaches flight, with one wing of healthy scepticism and one of openness. In any new approach, including those in this book, we should be thoughtful about its value and just how we will apply it in our context, but this must be balanced with a strong selection of possibilities and opportunities. I would urge you to experiment and use the language of alignment in your team and organization, to test it and notice the differences that you will undoubtedly see.

Throughout this book, I will support these insights with case studies comprising interviews with business leaders and experts who have found success through the ALIGNED® model. Their stories will highlight how this model is adaptable and effective for organizations of any size or sector. We start with Dominic Jones, CEO of the Mary Rose Trust.

INTERVIEW   The Alignment Advantage in action
Dominic Jones, CEO, Mary Rose Trust

The Mary Rose *was a warship in Henry VIII's navy and was launched in 1511. She was the king's favourite warship, forming part of his 'army by sea'. She would go on to fight in wars against France and Scotland in a career spanning 34 years.*

The Mary Rose *was raised from the bed of the Solent in 1982, and the Mary Rose Trust is a charitable trust that is responsible for conserving and displaying her hull, and her unique collection of artefacts, for this and future generations.*

The Trust is also responsible for developing the museum as a world-class visitor experience and as a scientific and educational resource. The President of the Mary Rose Trust is HRH King Charles III, who has been involved with the Mary Rose *ever since his first dive on the wreck back in 1974.*

Dominic Jones is the CEO of the Mary Rose Trust, and here he outlines how he has gained the Alignment Advantage for his organization.

The ALIGNED® approach has made my job as a new CEO easier, as I am able to deliver strategic and cultural change quickly and collaboratively with all stakeholders, from volunteers to board members. We have been able to drive change through within a six-month period rather than a long, drawn-out three-year process.

So the first advantage is that the ALIGNED® approach has probably saved us about three years of work! It has meant that everyone in the business, from our trustees to our volunteers and everyone in between, is clear on who we are, where we are going and what it will look like when we get there.

In a recent board meeting I took a step back and watched as our trustees and executives both quoted back the strategy and cultural narrative, and were using the ALIGNED® approach in order to make sure we created the right roles and recruited the right people for vacancies in our executive team. In the same week, during a walk of the museum floor, one of our cleaners came up to me and not only proudly showed me the Tripadvisor review about the cleaning, but also enthusiastically expressed how he is integral to delivering our vision and purpose. I hear it when discussing objectives with our duty managers. They are all keen to demonstrate how they help deliver our key strategic objectives.

What is so great about all of this is that we haven't even done an official launch yet. The ALIGNED® approach has ensured we are all working to-gether towards the same goal. In the space of six months we have achieved what would have been a painful, long-drawn-out, time-consuming process. It literally could have gone on for years and meant the business wasn't actu-ally delivering its strategy nor its purpose, values or vision. As a new CEO this approach has certainly allowed me to do my job well from day one.

The *Mary Rose* is coming up to the fortieth anniversary of the raising, and in that time has gone through a significant change in focus, from the raising to the funding and building of a new museum, and now looking towards becoming a world-class attraction. The Trust had traditionally been run like a project and over the last few years we made the change to a business which has been successful but, understandably, had some siloed thinking and mixed objectives at all levels. When I started it is fair to say that if you asked ten different people they would all say something different about our purpose and our vision and our key objectives.

The process of creating key strategic objectives and an ALIGNED® five-year business plan that delivers the objectives helped us all mutually agree which are the most important for the *Mary Rose*, and help define our strat-egy. During the process we reviewed our charitable objectives and put them front and centre again, along with four key strategic objectives. We set our-selves some ambitious yet achievable targets for 2025, and our strategy was complete. The next challenge was our culture.

An ALIGNED® cultural narrative was something that we desperately needed. Everyone had a different view of purpose, values and vision. We started with a number of workshops with everyone including volunteers, staff, managers, trustees and stakeholders. This gave us a shortlist of values that were important to everyone. From those, the Trust's values were created. Having a shared cultural narrative that everyone helped create meant that everyone was talking about it even during the process of creating it. Our purpose was essentially our charitable objectives reimagined and shortened into a clear sentence.

One of our senior staff, who was originally a diver who had helped to raise the *Mary Rose*, drafted this, which instantly got everyone's support and buy-in. The vision was more complicated, as it need to fit with, but be distinct from, the purpose. We needed to work out what the *Mary Rose* of the future would be, and this was agreed in a workshop with a mixture of constituents from all levels and all parts of the Trust. The cultural narrative quickly started to become part of everyday life, featuring in our five-year plan, presentations, awards and general conversations.

In the past I have worked in various businesses that have either been strategically and commercially focused, or primarily culture focused. I believe that giving one dominance over the others is a disadvantage. Having an ALIGNED® approach means that the organization can really deliver and operate at the top of its capability and potential. At the Mary Rose Trust, and thanks to the ALIGNED® approach, both the strategy and culture are of equal priority. They go hand in hand and have that symbiotic relationship that really works and enables us to create outstanding experiences for our visitors. I couldn't be prouder of the team and the organization, and it is worth underlining that, to understand and have the ability to talk about strategy and culture together has helped us come through one of the darkest periods in our history. We have moved quickly from a period where we were not even sure if we would survive the pandemic to a place where we have a five-year strategy, an ambitious future vision for the next ten years, and ongoing conversations about what it's going to feel like to be part of this incredible journey.

Of course, the impact on the visitor experience has been significant, too. The Mary Rose Trust has always prided itself on our visitors' experience. We have amazing Tripadvisor scores and customer service feedback. The ALIGNED® approach has meant we can let our visitors know more clearly what they can expect from the Trust and what the future holds for the *Mary Rose*. We can include loyal and regular visitors in decisions, and we can collate their feedback in an aligned way and continue to make improvements to our offering for future generations.

Thanks to the clarity that our key strategic objectives give us, we are focused on what we need to deliver for the next five years, and this includes a renewed focus on our visitors and how they experience our amazing collection. This has led to a virtual museum; a new immersive entrance depicting the sinking of the *Mary Rose*. We are now working on delivering a 4D attraction telling the story of the finding, excavating and raising of the *Mary Rose*. We also are now proud to shout about the amazing conservation work the team do. We will bring this into the museum and our marketing more as we drive to achieve both our strategic and cultural goals.

All in all, the ALIGNED® approach has helped me and the team to take some revolutionary steps, not just to secure the future of one of the world's most historical collections and attractions, but to create a compelling and commercially successful future that just a few years ago would not have been dreamed of.

The most powerful line in Dominic's story of grabbing the Alignment Advantage, is 'the ALIGNED® approach has probably saved us about three years of work!' Rarely do we talk about the sheer pace of change that can be achieved by applying the ALIGNED® methodology, but it is one of its great advantages. If you want to drive strategic or cultural change in your organization or you want to do a better job for your customers, then read on and apply the insights.

References

Meier, D (2000) *The Accelerated Learning Handbook: A creative guide to designing and delivering faster, more effective training programs*, McGraw Hill Education, London

Sinek, S (2010) How great leaders inspire action, TED, www.ted.com/talks/simon_sinek_how_great_leaders_inspire_action

02

The three key components of the ALIGNED® framework

For effective alignment, it is essential that everyone within your organization has clear, shared and aligned definitions of the three key components of the ALIGNED® framework – strategy, culture and the X. Therefore, here are the definitions that I encourage teams to adopt in the absence of their own.

Strategy

You will read more in the next chapter about my journey to understanding strategy and building strategic frameworks. It was a long and often confusing process, and when clarity prevailed I settled on this definition:

> Strategy is the overall key objective and the rich, multifaceted sub-strategies, actions and tactics that combine to deliver the key overall objectives.

It is helpful to adopt the view that if your strategy does not meet this definition, it is not a strategy. It is equally useful to agree as a community of leaders not to use the term strategy to mean anything other than that described above.

Every leader using a shared definition is a small but significant step towards gaining the Alignment Advantage.

One of my favourite realizations that developed and deepened my understanding of strategy is that, while on the surface strategy is brilliant for guiding the organization on what it should be doing, actually the most useful thing that a strategy does is tell the people in the organization what they should *not* be doing. If it doesn't contribute to the delivery of the strategy, don't do it!

Culture

If you were to ask people throughout your organization what is meant by culture, you would likely get a range of answers, including:

- how we act
- how it feels to work here
- what is important to the business
- how we treat each other
- how we all show up (especially the bosses)

In fact, organizational culture is a combination of all of these things, plus a little bit more.

It certainly includes how it feels to work here; what we will tolerate. It is often shaped and demonstrated by the decisions we make and don't make. It is also manifested in how we show up for each other and how we treat each other, especially when the pressure is on.

However, there is another vital component that is regularly overlooked. How we actually go about doing the work is as much an indicator of culture as anything else. The policies, processes and procedures you and your colleagues follow are themselves a gauge of your organization's culture, as is the degree to which they are followed or not.

The fact that these indicators combine to create the culture is why this is my favourite definition of culture:

Culture is how we 'be' around here.

This may not be a perfect use of the English language, but it is the most accurate way I have found to bring all of the facets of organizational culture together into one solid definition.

Culture is modelled from the top of the organization, but is created in a much more collective way than strategy is.

In Chapter 6 I will outline more about culture and what drives it, but it is useful to note that I have made no reference to purpose, values or vision so far. These are vitally important in the process of creating your culture, but they aren't the culture itself.

The X

In the ALIGNED® methodology and framework, the X encompasses two areas that overlap significantly when defined and executed property.

Customer experience

First is customer experience. Let me be crystal clear that I believe that customer service and customer experience are not interchangeable terms for the same thing. They have different focus points, will be created by different strategies, have different operational approaches and require significantly different types of measures and development for those people in customer-facing positions.

While I am a big advocate of customer experience rather than service, if an organization chooses to focus on service, there isn't an inherent issue with the choice, as long as they don't pretend they are doing customer experience.

Here is the fundamental distinction. Service is what the organization does with, to and for its customers. Experience is what their customers have:

Experience is visceral.

Experience is felt.

Experience is owned by the customer but must be curated by the company.

Experience is cultural, but service is procedural.

You can train your people to follow service policies, processes and procedures, but to enable your people to do what they need to in order to create the experience you want your customers to have requires your people to believe in the experience you are looking to create, and to be certain that the leaders of the organization believe in it too.

Brand

I will reiterate throughout this book that I believe that having clear and aligned definitions of terms you use every day in your business is vital in maximizing results of every kind. Brand is another example of the importance of this.

For many people, the term 'brand' conjures up a logo, a typeface or an advertising strapline. However, over the past decade or more there has been a huge growth in programmes that help to build an individual's personal brand. As a result of this, brand has become a term for presence, or how people or businesses show up. At the same time, many online gurus promise to help us grow our brands to X millions of pounds, dollars, euros, etc. In this case, brand is being used interchangeably as a term for a business.

As you will read in my interview with brand expert Ross Aitken in Chapter 10, it is vital to focus our definition of brand as:

What we do multiplied by what our customers feel about what we do.

When customer experience and brand come together and are defined and driven by an ALIGNED® culture, they become the X factor that distinguishes an organization from its competition.

More terms to be aligned on

You can probably start to understand how important it is to be aligned on the meaning of important words. Unfortunately, in almost every organization I work with, of every size, and in every sector, people are having conversations that are focusing on slightly different things. This causes as much confusion and misdirection as anything else.

As a matter of course, I highly recommend clarifying your colleagues' understanding of the following terms. Remember that it is more important that you agree with each other than that you agree with me, but these definitions have proven to be useful over the years.

- **Customer:** Generally the person who is buying your product or service. This is the most generic of terms.

- **Client:** Usually, the term used for a business-to-business customer. Where clarity is most useful in this sense is in agreeing whether the term client means the organization that is buying from you or the individual within that organization that is buying from you. Using this distinction wisely has made a huge difference to how we have defined, marketed to and served the people we work with over the years.

- **Visitor or guest:** If you work in the leisure, entertainment, attractions or hospitality industry, I urge you to consider what might be different when creating experiences for guests rather than visitors.

    For example, we first worked with Damien Latham, Jamie Charlesworth and their teams when they led the Leisure and Entertainments division of Majid Al Futtaim in Dubai. Their attractions reached across the Gulf Cooperation Council (GCC), including Egypt, Bahrain and Kuwait. In one of our early conversations about creating a unique experience for the people who visited their attractions, Damien made a clear call that, from now on, those people should be called, and therefore treated as, guests. He said, 'shops have customers, petrol (gas) stations have customers, hospitals have visitors, we have guests'. It was a small distinction that raised the bar, and changed his people's thinking and the course of the project.

    Be clear and aligned with your colleagues. Do you have customers, clients, visitors or guests?

- **Talent:** In an increasing number of organizations, the term 'talent' refers to everyone who works there. Where once there was a Head of Recruitment, there is now a Head of Talent. In other organizations, talent are those people who are identified as having the right level of performance, potential and desire to move up to the next level in the organization and beyond. They are successors to their senior colleagues and potential future leaders of the organization. This latter definition is my preference.

I never undervalue those who aren't classed as talent. Every organization needs people that I would define as the 'backbone'. These are people who are performing well in their current roles but don't, at that moment, demonstrate the desire or potential to transition to more senior roles. You must motivate, engage and develop your backbone, but you will do this slightly differently to your talent.

Of course, talent management is a fluid process. Organizations change, as do people's life circumstances and desires, so there's no reason that this year's backbone can't be next year's talent, but the key point is that not everyone in your organization should be pushed to want to succeed their boss.

- **Staff, people, colleagues or constituents:** The term that we use to define the people who work in organizations should be seen as a cultural marker. The four terms I have chosen are the most common that I see and hear. 'Staff' suggests a more hierarchical culture. 'People' suggests that importance is placed on the human element, while 'colleagues' suggests a greater degree of equity. The term 'constituents' is less common and one I first came across in the book *The Leadership Challenge* (2022) by Jim Kouzes and Barry Posner, which remains my favourite business book of all time. Using the term 'constituents' underlines the sense that each person in the organization is a component part of its success or otherwise. On the relatively rare occasion I hear the term used, I can make some accurate assumptions about that organization's culture.

My aim is not to convince you to use any one or other of these terms. The most important thing is that you and your colleagues have your own clear and shared terms.

Few people and organizations have brought the components of the ALIGNED® framework to life more effectively than Helen Bull, the

Divisional Director of Legoland Windsor Resort. In this interview, Helen highlights how these elements worked together to transform the performance of the resort.

INTERVIEW   Legoland Windsor Resort
Helen Bull, Divisional Director

As the Divisional Director for Legoland Windsor Resort, Helen is responsible for the long-term resort strategy, financial targets and the operational running of the resort for both employees and guests.

Helen has been with Merlin Entertainments for sixteen years and has worked across all three operating groups (Midway, Resort Theme Parks and now Legoland Parks).

Helen joined from Diageo PLC, where she held a number of marketing roles and worked on a number of different brands, including Bombay Sapphire, Croft Sherries, and Drambuie in both the UK and overseas markets. Her responsibilities include brand management and strategy, partnerships and promotions.

In this interview, Helen lays out how she used the Alignment Advantage to turn the performance of Legoland Windsor Resort around.

How important was it for you and the team to be crystal clear about your strategic objectives?

It was absolutely essential. Coming into the business, the objectives weren't clear to everyone. As a result, the leadership team didn't necessarily know what they all should be doing and what they should be focusing on collectively. I think it's one of those things to be aware of as a leader. If you assume that everyone knows what the overall goals are, and you're not careful about alignment, you can quickly find that everybody is just going off on their own tangent.

So the time we took to actually get together in a room, talking about what we wanted to achieve as a team, and setting out the overall objectives and the key tactics and actions underneath each of them too, so we were all clear on how we were going to achieve them, was invaluable. It really gave us a platform to start working from.

It might sound simple, but it is worth remembering that we did this just after the hotels reopened having been closed during the Covid-19 lockdown. We never close, so to close was a huge deal. Then when we reopened, we went from closed to fully open, literally overnight. It would have been very easy not to spend a couple of days out of the business, but

I knew it was the right thing to do, and the downside of not doing it would have been much bigger than the short-term challenge of stepping out of the business together.

Obviously we didn't solve everything in one go, and we are still progressing, but in the process of narrowing everything we had to do down into, sort of, you know, six clear objectives that we agreed would give us success in our business really accelerated our progress as a business and a senior team.

The result of that focus was that we hit bonus for the first time since 2017. Narrowing things down so we knew what, out of all of the things we could do, we should take care of first was significant. The objectives definitely provided a good framework for us to build on and to work from.

Since setting them, we have tweaked them each year, but we aren't suddenly going back to the drawing board. That is an important difference that I have felt from going from short-term business planning to proper strategic thinking. We aren't ripping everything up and starting from scratch every year. The other important thing was, prior to me arriving, the team had three rough years. Trading was challenging, KPIs weren't achieved and there was tension within the team. It was clear something wasn't working and we needed to acknowledge that, and actually take action to align what we needed to achieve with how we wanted to be as a team. I have a simple belief that if you are working together as a team, you are going to achieve a lot more than if everyone is doing their disparate work.

When you arrived there was so much to work on. How did you decide what the areas of strategic focus should be?
The overall key strategic objectives (KSO) were pretty clear. Most of what sits in the KSO is agreed with the global leadership team for Legoland Resorts, so that was the starting point.

Next we agreed the key aspects of our cultural narrative and our guest experience proposition. We knew that, in order to deliver the numbers, we had to create the best day out for children from 6 to 12 years old. Once we had those elements in place, and we had full agreement on them as a senior leadership team, the process of identifying the six strategic pillars was relatively straightforward. While we didn't agree on the final six straight away, we brainstormed what they might be, and there were a lot of options on the table, but when it came down to it we could see which ones were going to help us achieve the strategic and cultural ambitions.

Once we had narrowed everything down into the six pillars, a lot of the other strands and options fitted into those six pillars. I think it is a useful lesson. You might have twenty different ideas, each having their own merits, but actually taking the time to funnel them down into the imperatives provides a framework for everything else that might be important to fit into. We certainly found ourselves in a process of saying, well if we want to do X, we need to do Y first. For example, so many sub-objectives and sub-strategies fed our need to achieve an average of 7.5 rides per guest. Again, it sounds straightforward, but in a busy business in a challenging environment, clarity is so important.

Changing the culture at the resort was so important to you that you developed and included cultural objectives as part of the strategy, and I know you have had some huge successes. What were the most important early steps that you took to start moving the culture?
We really shifted the focus and style of communication. You know that I believe in being open and transparent with my teams. We initially focused on the connection between the senior leadership team and the senior management community. We then collectively created forums so that the frontline team could hear what's going on. If the people who touch our guests most don't know what they're aiming for, how can they contribute?

I believe in giving autonomy, but that's only possible when we are all facing in the same direction. I want people to know, 'Hey this is what we are aiming for. It's alright for you to run with it', and in moments that matter take ownership and responsibility. We were only able to do all of the communication and engagement pieces because we were clear and aligned as a senior team.

We had a big kick-off day before the beginning of the next main season where we had the whole company there. We used that as a platform to build on what we had done the previous year and say, 'This is absolutely what we're trying to do this year. We are going to keep focused on the things that we have been saying are the most important things for the last six months. We aren't going to let things distract us. We are going to lead from the top and you must hold us accountable to that.'

A consequence of this is that people of all levels feel able to approach us and ask us questions. They really want to know what we think and let us know what they think.

The more we achieve, the more confidence people have that they can make a difference. The more of a difference people make, the more likely we are to achieve what we need to. That cycle is a big difference to the finger-pointing culture that was present when I arrived. I could understand why it was happening. There were historical factors at play, but I had to bring people together, broadening relationships between people and teams that perhaps didn't get on so well in the past. As the leader, it was my job to recognize where those pinch points were and help them to put things in place to ensure that they were talking and that they were working together. If issues arise we tackle them. There simply cannot be a blame culture.

How did you make sure that you as a senior team were modelling the way?

In the early stages of redefining and resetting our culture, we agreed a set of senior leadership team commitments. I think the question you asked was, what behaviours do we want our teams to demonstrate and how do we make sure that we are displaying them first?

An interesting part of the process was to explore how we would ensure that we would actually feel okay to pull one another up if we weren't displaying the behaviours. We did this before we agreed what they were. In that way, we knew that whether it was being respectful, whether it was being open and honest with our communication, or whether it was listening, or all of those, we were committed to doing what we said we would do to each other first. We don't necessarily talk about the commitments every week, but we do still have them at the top of our senior leadership team agenda so they remain front and centre. Every couple of months, I will lead a conversation focused on how we think we're scoring on a scale of one to ten against a particular commitment. If the score isn't a very solid eight or higher, we will examine why and what we are going to do about it.

We have definitely been on a journey as a team and while we aren't perfect all the time we have definitely come a long way. As a result, people are looking forwards rather than backwards and we are continually building on that.

I think that's the thing with culture. It doesn't just happen. It's not like a number, that you either hit it or you don't hit it. I don't think culture is like a percentage. You measure it through your engagement scores, but actually culture emerges from the intention and work that we all do, and we have to keep doing it. Our current position is good, judging by the mood of everybody in the resort, judging by the senior leadership team, our culture is growing and becoming more positive. Imagine leading somewhere that you knew people didn't work, knowing that everything was wrong and not doing something about it. I could not do that. That's why we, as a leadership team, have to keep setting that example. It's not just about how we act towards each other, but also showing people that it is okay to do A, B and C, to create the experience that we want to for our guests.

You mentioned the importance of communication and I know that you tackled the resort's communication challenges quickly and successfully. What can people reading this learn from how you did that?
Firstly, most communication problems are problems with listening. We need to pay attention to what people are saying and decide what the real problems are. We have to focus on those issues that if we solved them would they actually make a difference to our people or the guest experience. I think it's healthy for people to have a little moan when they are having a tough day, we all do it, but we must listen properly to hear what really matters and what the real problems are.

Sometimes people feel that communication is a problem because they genuinely don't know what the business needs or that they don't know what the projects are for next year. Those things can be fairly easily solved if we pay attention and understand what people are really saying.

I also believe in learning from the departments, teams and business areas that do communicate well. What are they doing and how can we replicate that in other teams and business areas?

From a senior perspective, being visible and approachable goes a long way. I couldn't truthfully say I know the names of every single person who works at Legoland Windsor Resort, but I am sure that most of them know me and I am proud that when I walk through the park, so many people are comfortable to say, 'Hi, how are you Helen?' I can't necessarily say all of their names back, but I know which department they work in and I'm able to ask how things are going. Again, this might seem simple, but I know organizations where people are afraid to say hi to the boss, and I don't know how communication challenges can be fixed in those organizations because the fundamental interactions are missing.

The leadership team members can model the way, and it is important, because if you are approachable people don't wait for a formal forum to ask what is going on or share an idea. These kinds of interactions provide invaluable data and we share them in our leadership meetings. It gives a real sense of what is actually going on, on the ground. We can also head off challenges, operational and cultural, before they really take hold.

This accessibility and approachability also allows us to give people ownership for communication too. If you want to know more about the holiday village that we are building, ask your manager. Or ask the next senior leadership team member that you see directly. We have all-employee calls, too; they are something we did during Covid-19 lockdowns, and we have continued to do them. We hold them at different times so anyone can join, and they shouldn't be restricted by the hours they work. Sometimes the concern with those types of call is that people won't ask questions, but we certainly seem to get lots of them and we are able to drill down into why some of those questions are being asked.

On top of that we have things like Yama, which is our Facebook equivalent. We have screens in our staff canteen that are continuously kept up to date with key messages. So there are a lot of ways that people can find out information that impacts them or they might be interested in. We have a lot more platforms than we did a year ago, so while in the past the communication process may have been a little more about 'those that shout loudest', or maybe relied a little more on who happened to hear about something and whether they shared that information with somebody else, that is no longer the case. I don't think that people could accuse us of not taking communication seriously, or not doing all we can to listen and respond.

So, you approached the communication challenges you had as a cultural challenge rather than a process problem?
Absolutely. You discover a lot when you say to people, 'You're telling me, communication is the problem. What do you want us to do?' We implemented as many of the changes as we could. Eventually when we had all of these things in place, if communication is still seen as an issue, it tells us that maybe the culture isn't exactly where we want it to be, but also there is the possibility that communication can be used as a bit of a mask. Maybe it isn't communication and you didn't like the feedback you got or you just don't get on with a colleague. We are at the stage where we are tackling very specific issues, because the biggest issues around communication have largely been tackled. I am proud of that.

At its best, how would you describe the culture at Legoland Windsor?
At its best, the teams feel that they can impact the success of the resort. They feel that they have the autonomy to make a difference. Our people are

passionate about the resort. Out of that passion comes a sense of possibility and a want to continually improve the resort and themselves. We have paid special attention to inclusivity. We want people to feel that they can be themselves at the resort. We have put some measures in place to support this, and 87 per cent of people feel they can be themselves, which is a really good start.

We want people to feel that they can have ideas and make those ideas come to reality. For that to happen there has to be a sense of openness, trust and respect. All of these things have improved and are making the resort a more and more positive place to work. This summer has presented some significant challenges. We have had heatwaves and fires, we have had the occasional issue with rides, but you can see through people's body language that they're holding on to the culture through it all. Everyone really has supported each other and been in it together versus thinking that's a hotel problem or that's a ride problem.

All of these things come together to make it feel like this is a good place to work. We had our end of summer party last week, which was very good fun, but more importantly, so many people were saying thank you to us as well. People pretty consistently said, 'There have been tough days, but you know, we are all here because we love it.' That is the Legoland Windsor Resort at its best. It feels like a partnership. There is less 'You can only do this' or 'You can't do that.' So they really feel the difference as we continue to say, 'It is your resort. You know what we have to achieve. What do you want to do next?'

I want everyone to feel this. I had a session with the engineering team. In the past engineers may have been considered 'old school', challenging to bring on the journey, and as a result they were treated in a certain way. I said to them, look guys, what do you need, what do you want? I can give you the support. I can give you the money, but ultimately you as a team are here because you are experienced, skilled engineers and we need you. You have to decide how you want to be. You have to decide whether you want to come to a miserable place to work or a happy place to work. You have to decide if you want to be part of the new culture. One of the team said that they won't be part of any of the resort socials because of the shifts they work. I said, fine, I'll give you some money, but I'm not organizing it for you. Decide what you want to do that would make you happy.

How does all of this cultural work influence the experience that the guests have?

Culture exudes through to the guest experience. If you are in an environment that you are happy in and that you want to be part of and feel included within, if you are in an environment where your ideas are heard and you see the success of all of those things coming together, then I think that is only going to translate itself to memorable experiences for the guests. I see it every day where people are much more willing to have the confidence to speak to the guests. They are more willing to look at things from a guest angle and then say, we might need to change this. We might need to do that. Ultimately that positivity and passion for the resort will come through in your engagement with guests. We have done a lot, a lot of work focusing on guest obsession. There are lots of training models, lots of sessions but you can do all of that, but in reality, people have got to want to put it into action, otherwise the investment is wasted.

There is no doubt in my mind that happy people make happy guests. That is why we invested in a revamp of our back-of-house and, in particular, the staff room. We spent a lot of money on it in relative terms but, actually, if you don't have the key starting point of people being in a nice environment when they're on their breaks or coming into work, then how can you expect them to care enough to create great experiences for our guests? Culture and all of its aspects exudes out to the customer experience.

Helen's approach highlights the impact of shifting the three levers in the ALIGNED® methodology simultaneously. She wasn't willing to wait to make an impact and, by galvanizing her leadership team, they grabbed the Alignment Advantage with significant effect.

Reference

Kouzes, J and Posner, B (2022) *The Leadership Challenge*, 7th edn, Jossey-Bass, New York

03

How to gain the Alignment Advantage

The importance of clear and aligned definitions becomes clear as you understand more about how to gain the Alignment Advantage.

Firstly, your team and organization must have clear and aligned definitions of strategy, culture, customer experience and brand.

Secondly, you must examine carefully the degree of alignment across the three areas. As I described in Chapter 1, very few organizations think about these alignments, let alone work to implement them, but if you do there is no doubt that the results will be outstanding.

Six questions to start the Alignment Advantage

If you are serious about creating an ALIGNED® team or organization, ask yourself the following six simple but powerful questions. The answers will give a crystal clear picture of the degree of alignment that your team or organization does – or does not – have.

1 What is strategy?
2 What are your key strategic objectives?
3 What is culture?
4 On a scale of one to six, to what degree does the current culture help you to deliver your strategic objectives?

5 What is the distinction between customer service and customer experience?

6 What is the experience that your organization wants its customers to have?

Here are the key points to note when you review the collective answers to the big six questions:

- What is strategy?
  - o How aligned are the answers?
  - o When we talk about strategy, are we all talking about the same thing?
- What are your key strategic objectives?

Clarity about the organization's key strategic objectives will vary depending on the level in the organization the individual sits, but each level should at least have a clear view of what goals they are responsible for delivering. If I work on the frontline, or if I'm a frontline manager, I may not know the overall EBITDA that the organization is aiming for over the next three years, but I should know what my team and department are aiming to deliver.

If the question has been asked of senior leaders, everyone should be crystal clear and aligned. If not, act quickly. If senior leaders are working towards different goals, the organization can't be operating optimally.

- What is culture?
  - o How aligned are the answers?
  - o When we talk about culture, are we all talking about the same thing?
- On a scale of one to six, to what degree does the current culture help you to deliver your strategic objectives?
  - o Anything that scores less than a five or a six should be regarded as a sign that some degree of culture change is necessary. Consistent scores of three and below indicate that the culture is hindering performance.

- o It is also worth noting that when there is ambiguity in answers to question number two, it is impossible for this score to be high. We cannot know whether the current culture supports the delivery of the strategic objectives if we don't know what the strategy is.

- o When this happens, it suggests that it is a nice place to work, but it doesn't indicate alignment.

- What is the distinction between customer service and customer experience?

  - o The answer to this question indicates two things – the degree of alignment in understanding about experience as opposed to service, and the value that the respondents place on customer experience.

- What is the experience that your organization wants its customers to have?

  - o How aligned are the answers? If we aren't aiming to create the same X, there is no chance that your customers will have the experience you want them to have.

  - o And if there is misalignment among your top team, there is little chance of those at the frontline of your organization being aligned in how they create the X.

Armed with this data, and a clear understanding of how the elements of the Aligned Advantage interact, you can start your journey towards becoming an ALIGNED® organization.

You may already be making these connections but in the spirit of clarity and alignment, here they are:

Strategy and culture

Your culture must be created to be a strategic enabler.

This means that the most important influence on your culture is your strategy. If your culture is not created to be a strategic enabler then it will get in the way of the delivery of your strategy.

This is not about whether your culture creates a great or nice place to work, but instead it's about driving 'the way we be around here' to help to deliver what your business needs to deliver. The first key influence on your culture must be your strategic intent.

Culture and the X

Your customer experience cannot outperform your employee experience

While your culture is an enabler of your strategy, it's also true that your customer experience cannot outperform your employee experience. Therefore, your culture must also be shaped in such a way that it helps to deliver the customer, guest, visitor or client experience that you want to create. Your culture will inevitably seep out of your organization and be felt by those who are buying your product or service.

Culture is the pivot in the Alignment Advantage

This is why culture is the pivot in achieving the Alignment Advantage. Culture is both an enabler of the strategy and also a creator of the X.

As you start to consider these three factors in an aligned way, you will see each of them driving the next. While all three are likely to be present in some form in your organization, if you are thinking about the alignment of strategy, culture and your X, for the first time there is a clear starting point.

You must have clarity in your strategic goals to help you assess whether your culture is right to deliver your strategy. After this, cultural clarity and alignment around your X tends to emerge concurrently.

One of my favourite examples of a leader grasping the Alignment Advantage for their organization comes from the education sector. In this interview, Daniel Nelson highlights how he led the turnaround of a school on the edge of special measures using the ALIGNED® methodology.

INTERVIEW Using the ALIGNED® methodology in an educational setting
Daniel Nelson

Daniel Nelson is the Principal of Walkergate Community School in the challenging east end of Newcastle. His previous headship was at Choppington Primary School in a remote area of Northumberland. As you will see in the following interview, he took the school, its staff, its children and their parents and guardians through a remarkable journey of change. Mr Nelson is as inspiring as he is challenging and is as straightforward as he is thoughtful.

The remarkable story of how he gained the Alignment Advantage for his previous school really doesn't tell the full tale, as he achieved results that many people told him were simply not possible.

How from an educational point of view has adopting the ALIGNED® methodology helped in an education setting?
Firstly having the X, the external experience part of the equation, as one of the focal points was a game changer for me and the school. On the face of it, it seems to be a much more corporate or business-like approach. I hadn't really considered it. Culture is something we talk about in schools but not the impact that the culture has on the external stakeholders. The focus on the X created the first shift in perspective.

Then the clarity that I gained when I realized just how much of an enabler that culture is, was invaluable. It is the driver of what we would traditionally call the school development plan, which is its strategy, but it is also an enabler of the right experiences for those external stakeholders. The fact that culture is the connecting cog allowed us to focus on what was really important in getting us to where we needed to go.

When all three of those elements are pulling with the same degree of force then it really does impact on performance and results. We developed a school strategy that was ambitious but not so ambitious that it had a negative impact on the staff. We were mindful of that because, again, we knew that the right culture had to be at the heart of everything that we did. I wanted people to be energized enough and committed enough to implement the school plan because that in turn would have positive benefits for the children. Going back to the first point, we realized we wanted to create the right experience for all external stakeholders and that included parents, governors and other visitors to the school, including Ofsted and people from the local authority. This made us a really outward facing school. (Ofsted is the Office for Standards in Education, Children's Services and Skills in the UK. Their remit is to improve lives by raising standards in education and children's social care. They inspect and regulate thousands of organizations and individuals providing education, training and care.)

The Aligned Advantage in our school came from exerting the same force on all three areas, which resulted in a smooth uplift in performance and results.

How do you start making cultural changes in a school environment?
In most cases I will start gradually at first, and, ideally, in ways that are tangible. For example, in my new school we have a celebration assembly each Friday, and I have helped the teachers to free up their time so they are all part of that assembly. Until recently, it was my role as the Head to be in that assembly, but by including all of the staff it sends a clear message about the connection between the teachers and the pupils. It is a joint celebration of the pupils' achievements. It is a shift in process, but it signals a subtle shift in culture and impacts the pupils' experience too.

When I shared with the staff this was going to happen I got brilliant responses from the teachers, teaching assistants and learning support assistants. It signals that we are all in this together. Some staff were due to oversee some guided reading but I said missing 20 minutes of guided reading is less important than getting this bit right. This signals a small, unspoken cultural shift. It shows that we care more about the success of the pupils at the school than shoehorning in one more piece of work.

What did the strategy look like in your last school? What did that school plan focus on primarily?
In most schools their plan will be known as the school development plan, but I consciously used the term school strategy because I wanted to signal that we were taking a different approach. Being different strategically, culturally and in the external experience, is important if you want to create different results. Ofsted's highest measure is 'outstanding'; to me, that means doing things that make you stand out. My mum had a mantra which was, 'Why be a pigeon when you can be a flamingo?' and that is something that I try to carry into my work and life.

We started our strategic process by shaping the top two tiers of the strategy. These tiers clearly laid out what we had to achieve and what we would measure our success against. While I led this, I involved my senior team in the process to make sure I had their input and that we were all aligned in our thinking.

As part of the process, we would also involve staff from across the school to gauge where they thought we were. I think this input from staff is so important. I would regularly ask, 'Are you sure that's what you think? Can you give me some examples?' The aim wasn't to challenge them as such, but instead to be sure that we were all aligned in our thinking about the starting point for the strategy. I know that some people think that strategies are built to solve problems. Well our school strategy was built to bridge the gap between where we were as defined by me, Ofsted, the governors and the staff, and where we wanted and needed to be.

You mentioned Ofsted. To what degree did the Ofsted framework influence your strategy?
It was definitely one of the inputs. One of our key deliverables had to be improving our Ofsted grading. When I arrived, the school had been inspected and deemed to be 'requires improvement'. So while it wasn't the only strategic measure, moving to 'good' on the Ofsted framework had to be one of the measures. As we built the plan to achieve this, we found more that we would judge ourselves, self-evaluate ourselves and measure our progress against. In the three-year period I was at the school, we moved from the lower end of 'requires improvement', to the higher end of 'good', which was a brilliant achievement for everyone involved. For anyone not familiar with the grading scale, the next level above good is outstanding, and it would have been incredibly challenging to achieve this in the area that we were in.

From these conversations with our senior team and the staff as a whole we shaped what I called our gold standard. This is what you would call the key strategic objective. It included having a balanced budget and achieving the 'good' Ofsted standard.

From there we shaped our strategic pillars. Initially there were four, but as we reviewed them to ensure that together they would lead to the delivery of the gold standard, we added a fifth. It is worth saying that the addition of the fifth pillar, which was 'creating a broader, more balanced, curriculum', emerged during conversations with staff.

Parental engagement is another of the pillars that wouldn't have emerged if we hadn't followed the process that we did. It was hugely valuable. We ended up with five strands that we believed would drive us towards a good Ofsted and a balanced budget.

When we then pulled those five strands down into a series of sub-objectives and action plans, the process left us with specific steps showing how we're going to get to where we need to get to and how we would evaluate our progress. We could also see who was in charge of which stream of work and, in some cases, how much it was going to cost.

The strategy was set over a three-year cycle, which felt like the right time frame to have the impact that we wanted to. We didn't want to create something that we had to fully reset every twelve months. For example, in order for us to deliver when we needed to in the learning and teaching strand of the strategy, we had to first develop our middle leadership to enable them to make the changes required to our curriculum.

The process of breaking down these three-year goals became less onerous than I would have initially thought. In each year of the three-year cycle, there are three terms, so we set a progress point, a goal, that we should have achieved at the end of each term. Very quickly we moved from what were big, ambitious goals to having nine milestones that were achievable and that were a clear guide to keep us on track.

Some people reading this may feel like this is very hard work and a lot of time was spent thinking instead of doing.
It is a short-term view. This is a situation where you have to do the work up front. Investing the time up front saves so much pain in the long run. It is like any high-performance activity – we have to be ready to put the hard yards in if we want to produce the best performance. If we as educators aren't willing to do what is required to produce the results we want, how can we expect our pupils or their parents to do so?

In addition, that investment of time, energy and thinking ensures that the workload isn't overly onerous in the long run. In turn this has a positive impact on the learning culture in the school. For example, I felt a shift when people realized that every deliverable and every action had an end date and an owner. Everyone involved in the strategic process knew that we were serious about making progress and that was a positive thing. They could also see clearly what success looked like. If anyone was in doubt that we were about to do something differently, then those doubts had been dispelled.

What are the key challenges that you have faced in shaping the culture to support the delivery of a school strategy?

The most obvious lesson is that it is really hard to get people to live the culture. I realized that my perception of what our values stood for was different from other people's. We built the values into our performance management, but I still found it quite tricky to define clear examples of what being respectful – respect being one of our values – looked like and what not demonstrating respect looked like. People have different stand-ards, different expectations, and it took longer than I thought it would to gain a degree of alignment. We had to have conversations where we agreed what living the values looked like. I was conscious that doing that initially diminishes the impact of the value as there is a risk that people feel like you are dictating how to act, but we had to create a baseline. Managing that was the hardest part of the process for me.

Despite the challenges, you were successful in creating a cultural shift. How did you achieve that?

The single biggest shift came from leading by example; by backing up what we say we are going to do by doing it. We said we wanted healthy bodies and healthy minds so I went first by finding ways to reduce workload for the teaching staff wherever possible. Of course when you're teaching, you're in the classroom, but I thought there was an opportunity to reduce the paper-work teachers were completing. Myself and the senior team focused on how we could lessen the load and provide time for the administrative tasks that had to be completed.

It says so much more if I show that I respect you. I want to show that you belong. I want you to be happy in school and I want you to be healthy by reducing your administrative burden. I showed that I was living the culture which meant there was little option for them but to do the same. That is not to say that worked every time because it didn't, but when we had our suc-cesses that was at the heart of those successes.

Tell us more about how these cultural shifts influenced the external experiences you created.

When we first started talking about external experience, I initially felt like it was more relevant to businesses that have clients or customers. I think of your work with Merlin. They have visitors to their theme parks and attrac-tions. And as I reflected on that I realized that we have people coming into our schools all of the time.

The most obvious are our children and their parents and guardians. Of course we want to create great experiences for them. They are our bread and butter and the reality is that we are paid approximately £3,000 per student, per year to give them a great educational experience.

Once I was in that way of thinking, it very quickly broadened out to consider the experiences we want to give our other external stakeholders. How do we want our governors to feel? At a superficial level we want them to feel warmly welcomed, and that we are ready and prepared for their visit. We don't want them to feel like we have forgotten they were coming, which is some feedback that I had from a governor in one school I worked in. We have sports coaches who visit regularly from the likes of Newcastle United. When they arrive how do they feel, and how do they think that we feel about them being here? Again, in my new school there was some feedback from one of the coaches that he didn't feel like we were sure which year group he should be working with. That isn't the experience that I want that external stakeholder to have. We can add the likes of Ofsted to our list of external stakeholders, contract firms who regularly visit the school, and other support agencies. I quickly changed my perspective that having a defined external perspective was more a thing for business than for educational establishments, but I want to clearly define what the experience is we want those stakeholders to have, and work out how we best make that happen.

To go back to the question, of course the culture plays a huge part in the creation of those experiences. The biggest part in my view. Pupils, parents, governors, Ofsted, support agencies all feel the culture when they visit, or even when they receive an email. So, as we define the culture, we had to make sure that we were creating something that we would be happy for these stakeholders to feel.

If there was one key factor in your application of the ALIGNED® methodology that helped move the school from where it was when you joined, to where it was when you left, what would that be?
When I joined the school, it had been inspected and judged 'requires improvement', and many people consider that it was likely to be at the low end of that category. There were no systems in place. The culture was undefined. The experience the pupils were having wasn't what it should have been. Things were pretty rock bottom, so I knew that any change I was going to make would be positive. Despite that, it was still somewhat of a

surprise that the thing that created the biggest shift was that we got our external message right.

We engaged with the stakeholders that we thought make the biggest difference first. We had a series of meetings with parents and listened to what they told us. This included the sense that the school doesn't offer very much in the way of extracurricular activities. They told us that they had been kept at arm's length. We listened and did simple things like opening the doors and welcoming them in. We showed them quickly that we had a plan to broaden the school's activities. We didn't do everything straight away, and there were some things we never did, but fundamentally they wanted their kids to have a better experience at school and we gave them that. We put effort not only into what happened in the classrooms, but also into what was going on outside the classroom. As soon as they saw we were doing that, they were on the journey with us. Having the parents on board made a huge difference. The staff felt more supported, and we wanted to do more and more. We built a custom bike track. We put a forest school area in the yard. We had a climbing wall. We put activities on in the summer holidays and after school. There were after-school clubs every week. There were after-school clubs happening at lunchtime, after school, even some at breakfast club. We transformed the offering and the external experience. It was more rounded and the kids loved coming into school, and the parents loved sending them in.

Over time we started providing courses and activities for the parents. We helped set up a community organization to support what was going on at weekends, so this wasn't just about being a school, it was about making the school the centre of the community, and that was integral to what we did. We were then in a place where it was so much easier for us all to have conversations with parents, which in turn made it so much easier for us to implement the part of our strategy around changing the curriculum.

Just to make the point again, the biggest difference came through the definition of a new approach to external experience. It made everything else easier.

So while your strategy shaped your culture and the culture shaped the external experience, as you started to bring the external experience to life, it supported the embedding of the culture and therefore the delivery of the strategy.

Absolutely – this whole methodology is mainly a process of pulling levers to make small little changes. These small little changes affect the culture without me saying, 'Hey we're changing the culture.' Culture launches don't work, but the conversations that I have with staff constantly shift their thinking. In my new school the conversations that are about the children being at the centre of what we're doing are constant. To support that we are making three quick changes that will make the external experience better, including the introduction of ClassDojo, which is a communication tool for the parents to help the children have a better experience. We are changing assemblies. We are bringing in a full menu for school lunch; at the moment they just get one option and we are changing this to four options. These are changes that people will think sit under the X in the ALIGNED® approach, but I need to show the staff that the culture that I'm talking about is being brought to life. The changes are as much about me showing that I am serious about that culture as anything else. In turn, I will see who in the team are ready to come on the journey with me. I want to build a talent factory. We need to identify and develop the leaders of the future and I will see who is right culturally in their responses to these changes. Developing more leaders will help me deliver the strategic goals. All the elements are interacting, and already in my new school we are starting to see the Alignment Advantage coming to life.

The journey that Daniel Nelson took his staff and students on shows the acute power of applying the ALIGNED® methodology boldly. His first intervention to align his senior team was on day one of this headship; in his mind there was no time to waste. Rarely will the time to make strategic and cultural change be just right. When it comes to grabbing the Alignment Advantage, the most important step is often the first.

04

The strategic starting point

The biggest challenge for many people when it comes to strategy is defining it. Hopefully, we have tackled that in Chapter 2.

The next biggest challenge tends to be 'Where do I start?' Partly, this is created from the first challenge. Trying to build a proper strategy from an ambiguous vision is incredibly difficult. Instead, the starting point of a strategy must be a clear key strategic objective that is SMART and captures exactly what the team or organization wants or needs to deliver. Before we delve into what constitutes a key strategic objective, I want to ensure we are clear and aligned on what we mean by SMART.

It is widely accepted that the SMART acronym was first shared in late 1981 by George T Doran, a consultant and former Director of Corporate Planning for Washington Water Power Company. Over the years, there have been various interpretations of the acronym, with the 'A' most commonly used to signify 'achievable'. However, this often causes confusion due to the challenge of distinguishing between achievable and realistic.

In the context of creating strategic objectives, the version of SMART that I have found to be the most useful, and that I would recommend you use, is:

- **Specific:** What is the specific deliverable?
- **Measurable:** Does the objective confirm the measure of success?
- **Achievable:** Is this objective achievable, given the timescale outlined?

- **Relevant:** Does the objective deliver everything that we want and need to and no more?
- **Time-related:** Specify when the result must be achieved.

It is probably worth noting that while SMART objectives were defined as such in the 1980s, the objective-setting process was most commonly associated with Peter Drucker and his management by objectives (MBO) concept, also known as management by results (MBR). In his 1954 book *The Practice of Management*, Drucker outlined the process of defining specific objectives that can be conveyed to all members of the organization. Drucker described the process of sequencing objectives, which allows managers to split work into manageable steps. This approach was seen to result in a calm, yet productive, work environment.

You will see the relevance of this thinking, and its brilliant simplicity, as we continue to demystify the strategic process.

Defining your key strategic objective

Unless you are a new business starting from scratch, it is unlikely that you are beginning from a zero base when developing your key strategic objective. Even in the largest of organizations, the key strategic objective is likely to be heavily defined by your investors or the market expectations. In many cases, your objective can look like the previous strategic goals + X per cent. While I'm not advocating that as the very best approach, it is the reality in most organizations.

If we define the key strategic objective as the ultimate deliverable you and your leadership colleagues are charged with achieving, then your footholds and starting points will likely emerge. That said, if you are a start-up business, a new team, or function in an organization, I can't stress enough the importance of proper research, analysis and diagnostics before you develop your strategy, and certainly before you commit to any significant investment – financial or otherwise. Despite what the adherents of 'starting with why', and 'build it and they will come' may say, I have seen far too many businesses fail due to a lack of understanding of market share and demographics, and the absence of even simple commercial research.

From a departmental or organizational function perspective, your role profile or job description might give you a steer as to what your organization expects you to deliver, but don't assume that, just because your organization has hired you as the new marketing director or HR director, other senior colleagues will automatically see the value of your appointment. Nor is it guaranteed that they will know how your team's work contributes to the organization's commercial success.

You will still find people who perceive the likes of HR and marketing as being an unnecessary cost to their business. It is easy to dismiss that as being old-fashioned thinking, but what if that perception is born out of a lack of strategic insight from those leading functions where value-add isn't immediately obvious? After all, a marketing team that produces digital content without clarity about how that content will move people through a sales funnel will always look fluffy to a seasoned sales director who constantly measures, or is measured, on cold hard financial results. Nor will an HR team who seem to spend their whole time introducing policies that make it hard for the rest of the business to hire and fire the people they want to ever get the respect that a competent finance team will.

These statements are filled with generalizations, but if you have worked in a large organization for any length of time, you will recognize them. One sure-fire way to ensure that people take you seriously as a leader in any organization is to do the required analysis and diagnostics to build a solid key strategic objective and subsequent strategy. Here is an example of this in practice. It is closely based on a real-life scenario.

INTERVIEW BUILDING A STRATEGY

Claire is a talented and energetic HR director. The organization she works in has a growing annual turnover of around £200 million. However, the organization does not have an aligned strategy but instead a series of operational business plans that mean that its various business units operate in silos and often compete with each other. Claire's challenge is a frequent one among the coaching clients with whom I work. She wants to build a strategy to help solidify and underpin the value that the HR team add to the business. However, in the absence of a group strategy, it is challenging to create a key strategic objective that connects HR's results to the organization's results.

Claire would rather build a key strategic objective (KSO) that draws together a range of HR measures, with a particular focus on engagement, retention and resourcing. However, while these things will undoubtedly add value, the CEO's primary focus is on the growth of the top and bottom lines. So instead, Claire decides to work with her colleagues in operations and finance to agree a commercial target. This is a percentage over the HR budget that they will add to the business, and Claire shapes this into a KSO.

The draft KSO that she presents to her CEO and CFO looked like this:

By the financial year end, we will provide a 109 per cent return on the agreed HR budget.

The specificity comes from the 'agreed HR budget'; the measurement is 109 per cent return. Claire feels it is achievable based on the budget that was agreed upon. However, she also makes it clear that she could deliver a higher percentage ROI with an increased budget. It is completely relevant based on the organization's commercial goals and current operating model, and the financial year end gave a solid timeframe.

Not only does this provide a starting point for the HR strategy, but it also changes her colleagues' conversations about HR. Suddenly HR becomes an investment rather than a cost.

Claire also has a clear starting point from which to develop her strategy. While there are more things to do than the available resources allow, she now knows that she must focus on the activities that will add value and those that easily demonstrate a clear return on investment.

More examples of key strategic objectives

The fast-growing multinational

In my early days working with the ALIGNED® philosophy, I worked with a global market leader in baby products. In their core markets, they were the best-known brand for dummies (soothers), baby bottles, sterilizers and other related products. A large Chinese insurance company had bought them, and their strategic intent was clear. Over five years, they had to double their top line (sales revenue) and bottom line (net profit).

This gave the structure for a clear KSO for the business. By X date (end of financial year in five years), we will deliver an annual sales revenue of Y and an annual net profit of Z.

Clearly, there were increments along the way, but the nature of the investment by the parent company made the delivery of this objective the most important by far.

The small but ambitious lifestyle business

Just because an organization is small, and doesn't have ambitions to be sold or attract investment, doesn't mean it shouldn't have a robust strategic intent. For example, another organization I worked with closely wanted to create a solid strategy to help them be more focused in how they worked as demand for their services grew.

During the coaching conversation, several elements emerged as being important to the managing director in the success of their business:

- increased turnover year-on-year
- maintenance of a strong margin
- launch of a limited number of new products
- integrity of their culture and client experience.

Based on their understanding of their business, market place and the potential challenges of over-committing, they crafted this KSO:

> When we have launched four consolidated products across the world, generating £700,000 at 62 per cent gross profit while living our culture and delivering on our client promises by 31 December 2023.

This gave a clear direction for their two-year strategy and made the development of the next level of their strategy reasonably self-evident.

Starting strategic objectives with the phrase 'When we have' gives them even greater clarity and energy, and makes them feel solutions-focused. It will of course require us to define in the subsequent enabling objective how specifically we will measure 'living our culture'. You may also notice the language of this key strategic objective is quite specific.

I first saw the phrase 'When we have' used by my brilliant former colleague Trevor Durnford. He was a master of helping clients to build their change capability and could blend a range of change tools together in the most powerful way to deliver exceptional results. He would encourage programme managers to write the milestones in their project plans using solutions focused language and always with 'When we have' at the beginning. The impact was immediate, and I make no apologies for standing on his shoulders and copying his approach.

To be crystal clear, starting objectives with 'When we have' through every level of a strategy makes the objectives clearer and more powerful, and it makes it easier to develop the level of the strategy that sits below each specific objective.

Here is an example of what to avoid. Here is the KSO for a marketing strategy:

- Design and implement multichannel marketing strategies to create awareness of our products and brand.
- Create promotional activities that increase market share.
- Develop a high-performing team of industry-leading marketing specialists.

Is this well intended? Absolutely. Is it SMART? Absolutely not. Does it give us a clear picture of the challenge, opportunity or deliverable? No. Does it build the credibility of marketing as a valuable commercial function? Sadly not. In fact, I would suggest it weakens its position as the chance of delivering value against these objectives is pretty remote.

Summary

Remember, the key strategic objectives are fundamentally the things we must deliver to make our organization, team or function successful. If we work in a department, or an organization, where it is more challenging to turn our deliverables into SMART objectives, it is even more critical that we go through the process.

A vision is not a key strategic objective and a KSO on its own is not a strategy.

INTERVIEW Strategy
Jonathan Gander

Dr Jonathan Gander has a unique and creative perspective on strategy. His specialism is the creative industries, and he has shared his insights with students at academic institutions including Kingston University, The University of Arts London and LASALLE College of the Arts in Singapore. He has provided specialist consultancy to organizations across the world, and in this interview, Dr Gander provides a concise, thought-provoking and occasionally challenging view on strategy.

How do you define strategy?
The straightforward answer is that strategy is a combination of assets and capabilities that are organized in such a way as to provide a competitive advantage – a way of working that rival firms cannot compete (profitably) against. This combination of assets and capabilities are the result of decisions involving investments and re-organizations that cannot be quickly undone or reversed. This should mean that rival organizations cannot 'dabble' and see if they can replicate the success of the strategic firm. This also means that strategy will involve risk, as these decisions are going to cost if they are wrong.

What are the most important or common mistakes that you see organizations and their leaders making around strategy?

The top five mistakes that I observe are:

1 Believing it can be done without risk.

2 Folding the strategy too quickly into annual KPIs. A strategy will involve investments and management attention that will very likely reduce the efficiency of the organization in the short run.

3 Calling everything strategic.

4 Convincing themselves that they actually have a strategy, they just didn't know it.

5 Allocating insufficient finances to the development of the assets and capabilities needed to execute the strategy.

What can leaders do to ensure their people have a shared view of what the strategy is?

Leadership must avoid 'apple pie' statements! If a strategy is something nobody can disagree with then it is a platitude and will be dismissed as management-speak and safely ignored as words not actions. It will be seen as a continuance of the normal practice, just in a different bottle.

A strategy must be memorable, otherwise it will be forgotten in the daily pressure of completing work tasks. Memorable means that the strategy has to have a degree of cost, be discriminatory; in other words, it must involve stopping doing something. A strategy must involve uncertainty and be based on a question that people in the firm recognize as essential to find the answer to.

How should people ensure that their strategic objectives are 'right'?

All strategies look right if they are separated from the actions needed to be taken to implement the strategy. It is only when managers specify what a strategy means in terms of implementation that the question that the strategy is attempting to answer is revealed.

Who can argue against, say, expansion into a growing geographic market, or a focusing of the product range in order to increase quality, or investment in new technologies in order to develop new products? Leaders must avoid the temptation to say 'First we develop the strategic objectives and then we pass it down the organization to work out implementation.' Instead, those developing the strategy need to pivot directly to implementation to sense-check the wisdom of the strategy and its objectives. Strategy and implementation are two sides of the same coin and all part of the same system.

How should a leadership team ensure that their strategy is aligned and delivers what it needs to? (The premise for this question is that I see so many organizations that develop a reasonable strategic objective, then sit a range of divisional 'sub strategies' underneath it that don't actually contribute to the delivery of the overall strategic goal.)
Well you certainly don't do that by cascading down objectives to the divisions. That is how you turn a strategy into 'business as usual but with a new name'. It is also how you set a strategy and then are confused about why nothing changes.

I strongly believe that senior leadership must not regard details as something that they couldn't possibly know about, and therefore must be delegated to their direct reports and their direct reports, and on and on. I believe strategic leaders do not separate themselves from implementation. They say, 'Tell me how it works.' They engage with the tactics.

What is the one piece of advice that you would give leaders around strategy?
Organizations and the working lives of most employees revolve around giving answers, demonstrating to line managers that they know what they are doing, that things are under control and progress is being made. That's fine, and understandable, but it's not the conditions in which a winning strategy is discovered.

For a winning strategy to be discovered, leaders need to trust their employees and allow them to be more like what they are outside of work. Outside of work they say, 'I don't know.' In their time outside work they say, 'I wish I could do this', or 'I wish I could be better at this', or 'Why do we always do this?' Leaders must create an environment that allows people to say 'I want to learn how' and 'Why don't we do this?' Building a strategic mindset in an organization involves letting people be human, asking questions, revealing doubt, and pursuing the new, that their non-working lives are made of.

Dr Gander's view is that strategy should be bold. Vanilla objectives, tackling everyday issues, communicated by standard cascades, just won't do. In fact, he would not categorize them as strategy at all. At the heart of his message is the deep belief that strategy requires commitment. Commitment to the process, commitment to the execution and commitment to the culture required to bring the results into being. As leaders, it is incumbent upon us to ensure that we have and demonstrate that we have that degree of commitment to the strategic process.

05

How to build an ALIGNED® strategy

I am going to start this chapter with a clear warning about what not to do.

When I work with groups of people who are developing strategy for the first time, around 80 per cent of them will make one of these three common mistakes:

1 Jump from the KSO to actions and tactics.
2 Create objectives that aren't linked to the KSO.
3 Focus the strategy on the areas of expertise or work that they are most comfortable in.

I will address these as this chapter develops, but you must avoid falling into these traps if you want to develop a full business strategy.

The best way to steer clear of these strategic pitfalls is to stay true to principle number 1 of building an ALIGNED® strategy:

Principle number 1 of building an ALIGNED® strategy: The development of the strategy comes from a systematic breaking down of the objective.

Let's take one of the example KSOs from the previous chapter:

When we have launched four consolidated products across the world, generating £700,000 at 62 per cent gross profit while living our culture and delivering on our client promises by 31 December 2023.

There is a very obvious way to break this KSO down into what I term the enabling objectives (EOs).

The financial results are going to be delivered through the launch of four products. If we assume that each product should generate the same income, the first four enabling objectives would be something like:

When we have launched product A in Z territories, generating £175,000 at 62 per cent gross profit by the end of Q1 2023.

The next strategic decision would be whether to combine the elements of 'living our culture' and 'delivering on our client promises' into each enabling objective, or to create a stand-alone EO for each of these two elements.

This particular organization opted for stand-alone EOs. They looked like this:

EO1 When we have launched product A in Z territories, generating £175,000 at 62 per cent gross profit by the end of Q1 2023.

EO2 When we have launched product B in Y territories, generating £175,000 at 62 per cent gross profit by the end of Q1 2023.

EO3 When we have launched product C in all territories, generating £175,000 at 62 per cent gross profit by the end of Q1 2023.

EO4 When we have launched product D in all territories, generating £175,000 at 62 per cent gross profit by the end of Q1 2023.

EO5 When our eNPS and NPS scores are consistently telling us that we are exceeding the industry benchmarks.

You can see that this systematic breakdown of the KSO gives a clear set of strategic pillars or sub-strategies for the period of the strategy.

If you are reading this book to develop yourself as a senior leader in a larger organization, then it would be fair to question whether the process is as straightforward when delivering many millions or billions of value rather than hundreds of thousands. Let me start with a pragmatic answer. If you follow the process, you will always end up with a stronger, more ALIGNED® strategy than if you don't. Following the process might not be easy but it doesn't have to be complicated. Before I focus on what to do, let's take a look at what to avoid.

Strategic fog

There is a very unhelpful strategic process that many larger organizations follow that makes it more difficult to deliver their strategic goals. Perhaps more importantly, this well-worn faux strategic path causes confusion, creates silos, stokes conflict and leads to double handing and double resourcing throughout the organization.

Imagine this scenario; the end of the financial year is approaching, so the senior team receive an invite to a two-day strategy event. They are asked to prepare a presentation of their strategy for the year ahead. Most members of the senior team think they should know what their strategy is and feel bad that they don't. One or two think they know what everyone's strategy is and so build goals and plans that reach beyond their remit. No one speaks to anyone else while preparing their presentation.

The two-day off-site begins with the CEO and CFO presenting the strategic goals for the organization. These resemble key strategic objectives, but aren't fully SMART. It is the first time that the rest of the senior leadership team have seen these goals. The team then go through the painful process of presenting and defending their faux strategies. Few of them have SMART objectives. Many of them have conflicting or duplicated sub-strategies.

The IT director presents their strategy, which includes a stream on hiring the right people. The sales director has created a project to change the way they reward their people. The HR director is going to implement a new learning management system – which is news to the IT director who has already outlined their plan to consolidate and integrate systems across the organization. The marketing director's strategy focuses on building brand awareness in new territories, which is news to the sales director whose new reward and recognition project is designed to increase penetration with existing customers.

Quickly the presentations turn into subjective cross-examination. The CFO becomes the chief prosecutor, and the CEO works to maintain an element of decorum.

Silos in organizations are more often a strategic issue than a cultural one. The two-day event ends with the team less aligned than ever, with few decisions made, and at no point has anyone, including the CEO, checked

> whether the delivery of the respective functional enabling objectives would result in the delivery of the organization's key strategic objective.

I have seen variations of this approach in so many organizations over the years. This well-intended patchwork approach to strategy creation is the root cause of numerous organizational challenges.

I would highly recommend you revisit the overall strategy and test its clarity and alignment if your organization or team are experiencing any of the following challenges:

- We have communicated the strategy, but people still don't understand it.
- We have multiple projects running across the organization that focus on the same thing, e.g. recruitment projects, new IT systems.
- We have multiple conflicting projects running across the organization, e.g. a systems integration project while new systems are also being introduced into the organization.
- Our performance management systems don't help us reward high performers or manage under-performers effectively.
- We have a problem with accountability. Each department blames the other when something isn't delivered.
- People rarely collaborate cross-functionally.
- Issues are always escalated upwards rather than individuals working things out with their counterparts in different parts of the business.
- Our organizational structures are excruciatingly complex. We talk about being a matrix organization but people believe this has just evolved because the structural challenges haven't been tackled properly.

This list isn't exhaustive; however, if you recognize multiple challenges on the list then a strategic review will definitely create alignment in how your organization operates and thinks. More importantly, the commercial benefits created by the Alignment Advantage will emerge quickly.

Strategic alignment

So, let's revisit the previous example and re-tell it in a way that is likely to inoculate that particular organization against many of the challenges above.

Let us assume that the key strategic objective has been heavily influenced by conversations between the CEO and the non-executive board. Because of this, the CEO can shape a commercial goal which they know will deliver stakeholder expectations well ahead of the deadline for agreeing the strategy. For illustrative purposes let us assume that this will be delivered over three years.

A two-day off-site is arranged well in advance of the deadline and all members of the executive team get clear direction on what they need to do ahead of the event. This includes:

- What the commercial goal that will be central to the KSO will be, along with a high-level view of the conversations that led to that number.

- What is missing from the KSO that would make you proud to be accountable for helping to deliver it?

- What are the key enablers that, when delivered, would ensure that we achieved the KSO?

- What will make our two days together successful in your view?

- What are the top three behaviours we must demonstrate as a team across the two days that will help us to achieve this outcome?

Ideally everyone's responses to the pre-event questions will be collated and shared.

Ahead of the event we would highly recommend establishing a toolkit of decision-making tools for moments where decisions need to be made but the way ahead isn't clear and obvious. 'The boss decides', should not be the default decision-making tool.

This set up allows a very different, richer, and more aligned, process to emerge.

Firstly, a conversation will ensue about the commercial target. This will ensure that each member of the team is aligned in their understanding of why that is the number, and whether this is an EBITDA, a growth number, a market position, a combination of these, or any other commercial objective. This aligned buy-in is the first vital cornerstone upon which the Alignment Advantage will be built.

Next comes the exploration of the teams' answers to the question, 'What is missing from the KSO that would make you proud to be accountable for helping to deliver it?'

Some teams will absolutely stick with the commercial goal and I am really supportive of that. 'When we have achieved an EBITDA of X by Y date' is a solid KSO. However, many of the teams I work with feel that it is equally important to balance the commercial nature out with some human elements. This often comes from a sense that delivering the number at all costs isn't enough. They want to deliver the number while striving to be better as an organization. In some ways, this thinking is the nucleus of the Alignment Advantage.

Back to our executive team event. The team will debate and dialogue the other elements of the KSO. Here, the importance of being unwavering about the SMART nature of the objective becomes extra important.

Finally, they settle on something like:

> When we have achieved an EBITDA of X, increased our overall employee engagement by Y per cent and maintained a net promoter score over Z by AB date.

For most organizations, committing to delivering on these three strategic fronts is more than enough of a challenge for any senior team.

Most importantly, the collaborative nature of its formulation means the team will be aligned behind it.

Breaking down the key strategic objective into enabling objectives

The next step in creating an ALIGNED® strategy is the systematic breakdown of the KSO into EOs. The combined achievement of the EOs should result in the delivery of the KSO.

If we head back to our executive team strategy event, the questions to start this process were also outlined in the pre-work. By exploring what the key enablers are that, when delivered, would ensure they achieve the key strategic objective, the team should dissect the KSO into the appropriate number of EOs.

The EBITDA objective is likely to be delivered by several EOs relating to sales or revenue, system implementation, and operations. The structure of the example KSO suggests a specific set of EOs relating to customer service and experience, while the traditional human resources or people EOs are likely to be split between being enablers of the commercial element of the KSO (having the right people in place to deliver what needs to be delivered) and the employee experience element of the KSO (creating the right environment that leads to a greater degree of engagement).

The process should end up with the definition and agreement on a set of enabling objectives that, when delivered, the KSO will be taken care of.

The team should be able to take a step back and agree that when we have delivered EO1 + EO2 + EO3 + EO4 + EO5 + EO6, etc., then we will have delivered our KSO.

In most cases, it will become apparent at this stage that not every enabling objective will sit neatly under each executive's directorate. This makes the whole approach quite different to that in the first example. We know we have a team who are exploring, in depth, who should own elements of a strategy, not based solely on job title, but instead on solid strategic thought.

A word on ownership

In short, every enabling objective and sub-objective in a strategy should have an owner. This does not have to be a senior subject matter expert in the area to which the objective is related. The owner's job is to ensure that the objective is achieved, but rarely to do all of the work.

If you are familiar with RACI, the process and project management tool, the owner would be the accountable person. In this framework it would be defined as the person ultimately answerable for the correct and thorough completion of the deliverable or task, and often the one who delegates the work to the performer.

Continuing the strategic alignment process

In the example I have used so far, the initial strategic alignment process was gained by the executive team coming together to develop clarity about the KSO and start the systematic process of breaking down the KSO into a series of well-formed, SMART and ALIGNED® enabling objectives.

To achieve this, including full ownership, during a two-day off-site would be a good achievement. A single executive event like this isn't the only way of getting to this point, but however the top level of the strategy is created, full alignment across the most senior team is vital because, of course, it is just the beginning of the process.

The systematic breaking down of objectives must continue in order to develop a number of sub-objectives until eventually you reach the point where you are defining specific tactics and actions.

Principle number 2 of building an ALIGNED® strategy: Build it down, execute it up.

The strategic framework is built downwards by the systematic breaking down of SMART objectives, ensuring that the objectives at each level of the strategy, when achieved, will deliver the objective above. When defining the strategy, it is vital to avoid jumping from the high-level enabling objectives into tasks, actions and tactics. All objectives must be owned, and all must have a timebound element.

This makes the process of execution more straightforward. Every action and tactic will, when completed, contribute in some aligned way to the delivery of an objective at some level of the strategy.

Is your organization too fast-paced to have a proper strategy?

Some organizations believe that they are so fast-paced that a strategy will be restrictive. Some feel that they are too busy to develop a strategy. These are risky viewpoints and indicate largely a false perspective. Most of the clients that I work with are incredibly fast-paced, fast-growing and complex, from theme parks to specialist hospitals, from innovative multinational technology businesses to entertainment organizations. Regardless of their pace, industry or geography, they all gain greater advantages when their strategy is clear and aligned.

There are two challenges in thinking that an organization is too fast-paced to have a strategy. Firstly, an organization without a strategy will always feel 'too busy'. A lack of an ALIGNED® strategy will always result in more projects pulling in different directions, more conflict, more silos, and more people working hard in different directions to achieve outcomes that don't necessarily contribute to the overall organizational goals. The strategyless organization will always be working harder rather than smarter.

Secondly, it suggests a fundamental misunderstanding about the evolution of a strategy. A good strategy will act as a pivot rather than a straitjacket. Or, to use another analogy, it is the anchor of the organization at that moment. Most people think of anchors as devices that stop ships from moving. However, it is much more common for anchors to be used as devices around which ships can move. They allow the vessel to hold or drift, with specific constraints depending on the conditions, and especially during storms.

This is the perfect lens through which to see strategy. Your strategy provides the direction as to what should and shouldn't be done in the organization. If a new opportunity arises, there are two fundamental questions to ask.

1 Does our strategy tell us that this is the right opportunity for us?

2 If not, do we need to change the strategy?

Number two should not mean a constant change in direction, but it allows those who own the strategy to have a serious strategic conversation about the opportunity. This is strategic alignment in action.

This is a perfect opportunity to demystify one final point about strategy. For many years I heard the term 'strategic thinking' and wondered what it actually meant. And in my work with hundreds of groups of leaders, I realized that almost everyone holds the mystique around the term and its definition. Strategic thinking is simply the process of thinking about strategy. A board defining what their organization's strategic objective should be is based on strategic thinking. The challenge of considering whether an opportunity aligns with the strategy is strategic thinking. An individual checking that their actions contribute to the delivery is doing strategic thinking. I believe it is time to demystify strategic thinking and define it simply as thinking about strategy.

06

The truths and
half-truths about culture

Several years ago, I hired a mentor. He had a similar business to mine but his business was bigger, he was charging more and his client list was one that, at the time I envied. I paid a not inconsiderable sum to spend time with him, pick his brains and learn how he had done what he had done.

He shared something that let me know that my investment in him was somewhat misguided, but that solidified my thinking about culture. He told me of his firm belief that organization culture could not be cultivated or changed. His belief was that culture emerged with people and the only way to change it was to get new people.

I didn't agree – and I still don't.

In fact, my work over more recent years proves that his view point was wrong, except in one significant way. Culture does emerge, but until the leader recognizes the degree of influence their behaviour has on it, it will always feel errant.

It is also worth me being clear now that I am a culture guy. I am passionate about strategy and customer experience, but for nearly two decades now I have been driven by a desire to make organizational cultures better. I firmly believe that creating the right culture is good for the people who work in the organization, better commercially, and better for the customers, guests, visitors and clients.

The main challenge in developing and changing a culture is the multitude of myths and misunderstandings that surround the concept. Here are some of the most important that I believe prevent organizations and their leaders from creating cultures that are aligned and hold firm in ever-changing organizations.

Creating a purpose, values and vision does not create a culture

One of the biggest challenges of culture change is the myth that it has been created. We have all worked in organizations who have spent huge amounts of time and money to create a purpose, values and vision. When they are agreed the leadership team share them on intranets and on cool merchandise for their people. Sometimes they will be launched at company conferences and during roadshows.

After that work is done, the assumption is that the new culture is embedded. After all, why wouldn't somebody engage in a set of values when they have been given a travel mug with them on?

Most organizations will have a cultural narrative which is a combination of purpose, values, vision and, sometimes, mission. However, the creation and agreement of this narrative does not change the culture, but for those involved in the shaping of the narrative, it often feels like the job has been done. Instead, it is just the tip of the iceberg.

Big bang launches don't work

Let me get straight to the point. When it comes to culture change, big bang launches don't work. In fact, as EM Rogers' work around the Law of Diffusion of Innovation (1962) indicates, a big launch of, for example, a new set of company values, will do more harm than good when it comes to creating an ALIGNED® culture.

In the following chapter, I will outline how to bring a new culture to life in a way that will make it stick, but it is worth highlighting at this early stage that the ideal goal when launching a new purpose, values, vision or combination of all of them, should be a slight sense of underwhelm.

By the time a launch happens, the new culture should feel self-evident, that to some degree it is already being lived and breathed.

While some people should feel like the new culture is aspirational, many should feel engaged in it and by it, and that many elements of it already exist.

The brand values conflict

I once worked with an organization that had a set of organizational values. They were pretty good. But they also had a set of brand values. Again, they were compelling, but they had little to do with the organizational values. Most baffling, they also had a set of people values. Again good, again different from the others.

No one could really tell me what the values reflected, why they were different and how they were connected. Yet people throughout the business were supposed to reflect them in their work. Needless to say, they didn't.

Having three sets of values is unusual, but it is common for me to work with an organization with a set of company values and a separate set of brand values. This is a sure-fire sign of misalignment between the internal and external faces of the organization. While some large brand houses may argue that their model of separating their brands requires individual values for each brand, I would still suggest a distinction between the values of the organization as whole and the identities of the brands.

Having more than one set of values always leads to confusion and diminishes alignment.

A good culture is a nice culture

I have made this point lightly earlier in the book, but it is really important to make it again as it is at the heart of the Aligned Advantage. Creating the right culture is not about making it a nice place to work. That isn't to say that I believe we should be creating organizations that are akin to sweat shops or driving businesses that don't care for their people. But always focusing on making it nice negates one fundamental human truth – everyone is different.

I spent some important formative years of my career developing people in call centres. At the time, the industry was reasonably fledgling and garnered some pretty negative press. To those outside of the call centre industry, it would have been easy to assume that those who worked there were living out their days in human battery farms. What I experienced was an environment that, for most of the people who worked there, was the most fun, most rewarding and most developmental of their lives. The culture was right for the people who worked there.

I have also spent time in organizations that cared deeply for their people, yet somehow so many of their people worked with a genuine sense of dissatisfaction. I particularly experienced this in the third sector, where organizations with a purpose employed people with a purpose but somehow their purposes were misaligned, leading to a genuine sense of discontentment.

The ALIGNED® methodology makes it clear that the right culture is one that enables the delivery of the strategy, supports the creation of the experiences that we want for our customers, guests or clients, and that we then retain and recruit people who are compelled and engaged by that culture. It is perfectly OK for a culture not to be right for some people.

With these and many other misunderstandings, myths and half-truths running around board tables and through organizations, it is vital that you and your colleagues are aligned in your understanding of the key components of a cultural narrative.

Purpose and values – the distinctions

Purpose

An organization's purpose should answer the question 'Why does this organization exist and why should anyone care?' The purpose should distinguish the organization from other similar organizations in the field, and, importantly, it should create a sense of connection for those people who work in the organization who share a similar sense of purpose. This connection, and the feeling that we as individuals are contributing to something beyond ourselves, is the real value of a purpose as part of a cultural narrative.

Earlier in the book I took issue with Simon Sinek's Golden Circle model and the message that it is the required starting point for successful organizations. I still firmly stand by that assertion. However, purpose is an enormously useful starting point for your organization or team's culture. Ideally, an organization's purpose should be crafted collectively by its senior team and, where possible, other connected key stakeholders should be involved in the process.

Values

Organizational values really are the cultural compass of the organization. They should outline what is really important to that organization and clearly describe the characteristics of 'how we be around here'.

An organization's values will ideally be representative of the most commonly shared personal values of the people who make up that organization, or at least of the people who lead that organization. If the organization's values don't reflect the personal values of the people who lead that organization then those leaders will not readily live and breathe their organization's values, and when that is the case it is almost impossible for the organization's values to come to life. When an organization's values are representative of the personal values of the people who lead that organization, then those people will be guaranteed to live and breathe the organization's values.

This alignment between personal and organizational values is vital but isn't the only factor in bringing values to life. I will share more in the following chapters; however, here is one critical and often-overlooked element. Your people will become significantly more engaged with your organization's values when they are able to have conversations about how they will demonstrate those values in their work and how the organization's values connect with their own. One brilliant piece of research by Jim Kouzes and Barry Posner (2022) found that when organizations launched new values without giving their people the opportunity to connect them with their personal values it could lead to a small decrease in engagement. However, when the constituents of the organization were able to connect the organization's values to their own values it could lead to up to a 20 per cent increase in engagement.

In short, it is vital to give your people the opportunity to talk about the company values, what they mean to them, and how they will demonstrate them in their day-to-day work. This presents a challenge for organizations that have a set of values, each with a further set of descriptors attached to them.

For example, we briefly worked with a well-established financial institution in the UK. They had shaped a set of values that they wanted us to help bring to life for their people. The process of creating the values had been reasonably good, with a cross-section of people from the organization involved.

Unfortunately, there was disagreement among their executive team as to the exact meaning of each value and, rather than allowing people to put their own lens on each value, they created a comprehensive set of behaviours that sat under each value.

This meant that the few thousand people who worked for the organization had 40 statements to align with (five values with eight behaviours under each), rather than just five values. Even more excruciating, many of the behavioural statements conflicted.

One of their values was 'straightforward'. You might agree with the executive team that this is a broad term, but whichever lens you might see it through would point broadly in the same direction. Living 'straightforward' as a value certainly wouldn't involve making things more complex. However, the detailed behaviours included phrases like 'have difficult conversations' as well as 'make processes as simple as possible'. By adding behaviours that created confusion about the value, the executive team ensured that the cultural change programme was already destined to fail.

The more you try to control people's interpretation of organizational values, the less likely they are to take hold and come to life. The more you allow people to make their own connections with the values and shape their own stories of what that value looks like in action, the more self-evident the value will become.

Values – language and number

How many values an organization should have is something I am regularly asked during conversations with clients. The truth is that there is no single right answer. In its heyday Tesco had just two simple values:

'No one tries harder for customers' and 'We treat people how they want to be treated'.

Shortened to customers and people, they were integrated into conversations every day, throughout the organization.

Merlin Entertainments, who for so long have been a paragon of cultural excellence, have seven values. These cleverly worded values, when connected with the organization's vision, make up 'The Merlin Way', which is a perfect reflection of the culture that the organization strives to maintain as it continues its global expansion.

My organization has three values: honesty, balance and connection. They are simple and straightforward, but mean something slightly different to each member of the team. They should be self-evident to clients, though.

Even in these three examples, the language and number of values are different. It isn't about a single right answer, but instead it's about finding a way of codifying the culture that you want and need to create in a way that is most likely to hit the mark for the people in your organization.

INTERVIEW Culture
Emma Woods

Emma Woods is an international consumer and brand champion who has moved from being a CEO to having a plural board career, supporting a range of customer-focused organizations at a pivot point to unlock their next phase of growth.

Her impressive career includes time as Marketing Director at Unilever, Group Marketing roles at Pizza Express and Merlin Entertainments, Chief Executive Officer at Wagamama, during which time she guided the organization through the extreme turbulence of the pandemic, and she now holds non-executive directorships at Huel, GPE and The Gym Group. She is also the Chair of Tortilla Mexican Grill PLC.

Emma has an exceptional ability to balance the need of the business, its people and its customers, while her humility and pragmatism enables her to bring people at all levels on the journey with her.

This interview gives a powerful insight into her thinking about culture and its influence on the customer.

What is your definition of culture?

Culture is a big concept, encompassing a very broad range of things, but in essence it is the way a society, a social group, a business, frames itself. What are our behaviours, our values, our core beliefs, the rhythms and routines of our daily interactions? In business, it is the context in which we understand what we are about; how we talk to each other, plan our next moves, and articulate our long-term mission.

Sometimes these cultural touch points are written on the wall or in handbooks, though perhaps if you need to write it on the wall I would suggest it isn't yet innate in your business. Culture should be something you feel, something you sense from the way a business talks to itself, its customers, the wider business community; a living, breathing, self-perpetuating presence that is nurtured by all under its umbrella. That is not to say, however, that a great culture will just take care of itself – it needs to be sustained and shaped along the way as things change, both internally and externally. This is the job of business leaders. For culture is an enabler of growth, and like any living thing it may wither and die without the appropriate care.

What have been the points in your career where you have had to focus on culture, either to maintain something brilliant or fix it because it wasn't right?

My background is in brands, so I have often been drawn to businesses where the customer proposition needs refreshing. As a starting point I always look back to the founder's story, because it is invariably there that you'll rediscover the kernel of why it was a good idea in the first place. You rediscover the spark. Understanding where a business came from can shed a revealing light on the problems of the moment and can lead to a new path.

When I joined Wagamama I discovered a very strong culture, which had been embedded in the business since its founding by Alan Yau. It wasn't written down at the time, but the team called it the 'Wagamama magic' and it was alive, you could feel it. It was a warm organization that welcomed everyone and also, importantly, welcomed new ideas.

At the time, we were growing very fast, so we wanted to codify this culture to really understand what was going on. In unpacking the history, we started to understand that the principle of genuine inclusion had been at the heart of the business from the very beginning. They welcomed self-expression among team members, with tattoos and pink hair very much a Wagamama norm, most unlike comparable businesses of the day. I also saw a creative restlessness running through the company, which I knew I needed to bottle and give a name to. This sort of progressive force can be incredibly powerful for moving a business forward; we called it 'zigging when others zag'.

These two cultural elements were there when I arrived at Wagamama, but they were too good to let drift – my job was to grow them, celebrate them and give them form.

Something that wasn't there when I arrived was Covid-19. A totally unexpected curveball can knock the wind out of a business, and Wagamama, being a hospitality business, was dealt a sucker punch when Covid-19 hit and we went into lockdown. How can we nurture a culture that is so invested in the vibrancy of the interaction between teams and guests when we suddenly had to close our restaurants?

A business with a strong culture should always know what it should do in any given situation. So, what did Wagamama do? Well, we may have been burning through cash like there was no tomorrow (and, frankly, who knew at the time?), but my instinct was to use our cultural imprint to keep the brand alive and well in people's homes, and give them something for nothing in a time of uncertainty. And so Wok from Home was born – a series of master class online cooking tutorials, hosted by our Executive Chef. The thinking was, if you can't come to us, then we'll come to you. The initiative really took hold and we expanded it to live link-ups to people's homes and guest chef editions. We zigged when others zagged. Even with shuttered doors the Wagamama brand and culture was very much a living breathing thing in the kitchens of the nation, making our customers aware that we were there for them, that we were in this thing together. Culture is not a passive thing, it is a guiding force for your business. Get it right and you'll know what you should do.

Another hugely important part of our culture is the notion that 'we've got each other's backs'. The pandemic was an incredibly worrying and un-settling time for the teams, as it was for everyone. Suddenly they were sat at home on furlough. Gone was the camaraderie and support of being at work – the teamwork at Wagamama is one of the great cultural markers of the business, but it was silenced in an instant. It was incredibly important to me that we kept the information flowing, so I recorded regular update videos that went to every single member of the team, keeping them con-nected and hopefully a little more settled. This sort of thing has become commonplace as a result of new ways of working brought on by the pan-demic, but at the beginning this was a new initiative. The team felt like the business cared and that the Wagamama culture remained the same no mat-ter what.

Lockdown was a crisis – the answer for our business was there in our culture and the values that underpinned it. So, in those moments when we felt lost because of this extraordinary set of circumstances, we looked to our cultural framework as a guide for our decisions.

It sounds like your culture was a cornerstone for you and your people, and, in turn this had a positive impact on the customer?

Absolutely. Being consistent about culture is so important because it is the framework by which the brand connects to the customers. It seems like another world now, but during the pandemic Covid-19 safety rules meant that businesses had to introduce screens, masks, distancing rules, etc. to keep everyone safe. The idea of keeping people apart is the polar opposite of the cultural expectation of visiting a Wagamama. So again, the question was, how do we zig when others zag? How do we do this in a Wagamama way? Part of the answer was in our innovative Japanese moveable screens. In most shops and restaurants, installing screens gave those businesses an unwelcoming air of an A&E department. Our screens were beautiful, with bespoke Japanese inspired designs, which could be moved up and down the benches to suit the number in the party. They actually felt like a positive addition, and importantly kept everyone safe. Again, this was a positive customer experience that came directly from our values and our culture. I think it's one of the reasons why we traded so successfully throughout those difficult times.

Was there any strategic or commercial conflict to doing this? You were making a decision that cost more, when there was huge financial pressure.
Every decision we made in that period was carefully considered, and of course the screens were more expensive than buying the more clinical versions, but if decisions are taken on a purely financial basis without thinking of the impact on either our customers or brand, then that is not good business. When our guests visit a Wagamama they do it, of course, for the food, but also for the ambience. Destroying that ambience would change the customer experience, so why would they come back? Maintaining the cultural fabric of a business is also to nurture its relationship with the people at the core of the business model: the customers. We were a business based on human interaction that believed in doing things differently, but we had to follow legal instruction manuals about how to serve food on trays and keep everyone apart. So we made a *cultural* decision that served our commercial and strategic goals. It was a win–win.

Have you experienced moments in your careers where culture and brand felt at odds with each other?
Not often. They should always drive each other. I am quite lucky in that my initial brand training was in Unilever. Now that I am older, I reflect on it and realize that there is a reason that Unilever has been around for over a hundred years.

Fundamentally the founders understood that they were there to serve their teams and their customers. There was a real sense of care for both groups. As a marketer there, you learned that your whole purpose in business was to make your customers' lives better. Luckily the culture there was very supportive, and people cared for each other. This then translates to the customer. It therefore doesn't surprise me that it's an organization that committed to sustainability goals ahead of other organizations or that it is more progressive in terms of diversity and inclusion than other businesses. A hundred years ago when William Lever founded the business there was a very strong sort of sense of social purpose; he built that into the culture. I have taken that ethos of aligning culture and brand forward to all the businesses I have been involved in since.

How do you balance your employees' needs with customers' needs?
Importantly, you have to measure both all the time. Ignore either one at your peril. What is clear is that a happy team drives happy customers or

guests, and that drives performance. There is a direct correlation. Happy teams generally come from great leaders. So if you've got stable, happy leaders who are clear about what they are trying to achieve and they support team development, you get strength and stability in the business. When you have strength and stability in the business, you get strong net promoter scores (NPS) and then growth. We used to find that there was around a six to eight week lag between the NPS improving and growth. And, equally, if the NPS goes down you have six weeks, ten at the most, before it starts going backwards. There was a really strong correlation.

Again, I think it comes back to your point that culture isn't necessarily this soft, fluffy thing. Maintaining the right culture requires lot of work, but when it is measured correctly any organization should be able to correlate staff turnover with team happiness and know that if they don't fix the problem then the customer experience will surely suffer.

This is especially important to track in strong leisure brands, as customers and guests return because of happy memories. Therefore they have high expectations, so if your team scores dip you have a very small window to fix the problem before your customer scores follow.

You have mentioned NPS as your preferred customer measure. Do you have a preferred way to measure teams and people?
Team turnover is a critical measure for me. I also believe passionately that two to three times a year you would do well publicized internal surveys where you really push to get very honest feedback from people. I prefer to get an eNPS score as well as qualitative feedback. The score gives us something to track but the verbatim comments are often the really useful thing.

If you are doing this as a leadership team, you have to be quite critical with yourself and use the feedback the people give you to change things for the better. In Wagamama we were proud of the inclusive culture, but following the murder of George Floyd we felt that we had to check with our people that we were as inclusive an organization as we thought we were. We created a survey that asked directly, 'We think we are dealing with racism, but what do you think?'

The feedback surprised us. Our work around issues relating to race and inclusion was very well received; however, it seemed that in order to protect our customers there were times when racism from customers to staff was tolerated. This is clearly unacceptable, but we wouldn't have known about it had we not actually asked them directly. This feedback allowed us to take immediate action.

And this particular feedback gave you important data about the culture but also how important the brand and customer experience was to them?

Absolutely. People are more likely to complete a culture survey when it is concise and the questions are relevant to their experience and their role. They also have to believe that the leaders are really listening and will do something with the feedback. I believe when we take action based on the questions that we ask our people it really starts to create a relationship and that in turn strengthens the culture further.

If you had one message for aspiring leaders, what would it be?

Ask yourself these two questions whenever you have a decision to make. Are you on your customers' side? Are you on your teams' side? They are the two most important questions. If you can demonstrate that you are genuinely on your customers' side, you will be in a good place. Equally, teams are under a lot of pressure to deliver for your customers, so we need to ensure that we are putting the right things in place to support and motivate them. The way you then answer and deliver on these questions should reflect the cultural backbone of your business.

Emma makes the clearest links possible between culture and customer experience. By tracking eNPS and NPS, she and her team could predict and head off customer challenges that could arise from challenges with teams in the Wagamama restaurants. Her experiences highlight brilliantly the impact and advantages of adopting the ALIGNED® methodology.

References

Kouzes, J and Posner, B (2022) *The Leadership Challenge*, 7th edn, Jossey-Bass, New York

Rogers, E M (1962) *Diffusion of Innovations*, Free Press of Glencoe, New York

07

Crossing the cultural chasms

Organizational culture change is treated by many like a corporate game of nailing jelly to the wall. You might believe that it is too difficult, and the chances of actually doing it makes it a process unworthy of real effort and commitment, especially when you have so many other things to take care of.

This chapter has two main intentions. The first is to give you a structure that, if you follow it, will help you bring your new culture to life in your team or organization. The second is to ensure that you believe that cultural change is more than a shot in the dark, and that following the process, diligently and with commitment, will get you the result you want.

You will see that, very early in the process, the commitment and belief of those at the top of the organization and those involved in the early stages of the cultural change is critical. If you waiver, your people will sense it and they will dip out.

Crossing the chasm

Having been around the periphery of full cultural change programmes for several years, my colleagues at TwentyOne Leadership and I decided to explore in detail what actually makes culture change stick in organizations.

We set up a modelling project to deep dive and compare the approaches followed by organizations that had started cultural change programmes and nailed the change by getting to the point that they aimed for at the outset. Vitally, we also modelled organizations that had started cultural change programmes and not got them over the line. We wanted to see what was missing from these programmes and whether there was anything extra that got in the way of these companies landing what they needed to land.

Our cultural change framework, which we affectionately called 'crossing the chasm', was developed from this modelling project and has been shared with and used in organizations on every continent.

This chapter lays out the process and steps to make your new culture stick and the pitfalls to avoid.

The business case for cultural change

Your organization has a number of strategic and commercial imperatives. Even if it isn't a profit-making organization, there are certain deliverables that must be met, and most things will take second place to them.

The first driving force for culture change in any organization is to make a clear and explicit link between these deliverables and the change in culture. Employing the ALIGNED® methodology as a whole will make this easier as you will have a clear understanding as to how the culture you want to engender will support the delivery of your strategy.

However, if for now we assume that you haven't made these links, it is vital to build a solid business case for the change programme. Do this in the same way that you would if you were about to invest significant amounts of money in a new IT system, or restructure your team or department. Involve your peer group in the building of this business case, even if they don't quite 'get it' yet. Show the financial, commercial and strategic benefits of driving the programme to completion. Position it as a burning platform. Show the pain that will be caused if the culture remains the same.

If you don't build this compelling business case before doing anything else, I can guarantee one thing for sure: *something else will become more important*.

I started advising one of Europe's largest energy companies several years ago. They wanted to embed safety into the culture of the organization in a way that had never been done before. A significant amount of cash, time and effort was set aside to drive a meaningful culture change programme. However, the director in charge of the programme had not created a strong enough business case for their C-suite colleagues. As the programme was gathering momentum, the latest customer data landed and, with it, a threat of a fine from the regulator. Overnight, the single most important strategic imperative (zero harm) became the second most important imperative. Soon after we stepped away from supporting the organization, we heard that the interim financial results were in and the programme was 'paused'.

I am not making a judgement about whether employee safety, customer service or financial return should have been the number one strategic imperative, but I am clear on the negative impact on the reputation of the leadership of the organization in starting a cultural change programme to embed safety into the culture of the organization, then canning it a couple of months in.

If you can't commit to the whole change programme, don't start it; and if you haven't built a strong enough business case, it is inevitable that something else that seems more important will be given precedent.

Define your cultural landing point

One of the most surprising insights from our project to understand what makes cultural change stick was the number of organizations that had started cultural change programmes without really defining what they wanted their new culture to be.

In some ways, this was the seedling thought that eventually developed into the Alignment Advantage. Leaders are willing to commit significant amounts of time and budget to achieving a 'better' culture, or becoming 'an employer of choice' or 'a great place to work' without really understanding what this looks like in their organization.

The moment I, or one of my team, ask the question 'When the culture at this organization is exactly as you would want it to be, how will you know?' the whole nature of the conversation changes.

Some leaders come alive. They are no longer talking about an abstract concept that may or may not make a difference to how it feels to work in their organization. Instead, they are beginning to build a concept that they can be emotionally invested in.

Other leaders shy away from the conversation for exactly the same reason. The sense that a new culture is something that they can shape, bring to life, and that they must lead, and it can feel overwhelming. Instead, they would rather go through the generic process of values on mugs and intranets that they have seen fail over and over again, but at least they can't be held accountable for something they were never invested in, in the first place.

The fact that you're even reading this book tells me that you want to do something different, so here are the three acid tests to apply when defining the cultural landing point:

1 If you hit that landing point, would it help you deliver your strategic intent?

2 If you hit that landing point, would it help you to deliver the X that you want to? (More on this in later chapters.)

3 Does what you have described excite you enough to sign up to finding ways to live and breathe it every day?

The initial landing point description doesn't have to be a SMART objective. It doesn't really even have to meet all of my criteria for an engaging vision, but it must be a clear enough description of the culture that you and your senior colleagues want to bring about that you can refer back to it throughout to ensure that the whole cultural change process is on track. As you will see later in the chapter, you also need to be able to link the very last stage of the process back to it too.

Here is an example from a client that I have already referred to in this book:

We are already brilliant and doing more with less, but to achieve what we need to over the next five years we need to be more innovative and creative. We are great at 5 per cent increments and 10 per cent savings. We need to be able to work together across the organization in a way that we never have before, to change the dial on our products and how we deliver them to our new markets. Our people need to know that we are serious about this, even though we as a senior team will find it hard. We need a culture that keeps the best of what has brought us to where we are now, the pace we work at, the desire to win, our brand positioning, but adds creativity, innovation and connection across and up through the organization.

They were crystal clear in what needed to stay culturally, what needed to change and, vitally, how hard it would be for them as an executive team to lead this new culture. If you create something like this with your senior colleagues, then you really will have taken a massive step along the cultural path.

Here is another example from a sporting environment:

Winning and together. That's it. Everything else either supports this or is peripheral. This club hasn't been together in nearly a decade. The people who run the club are divided, the fans are divided, the dressing room is divided. It's why we lose over and over again. Financially and on the pitch. But we are here to win. Togetherness will lead to winning, but if we aren't winning, we won't be here. If we asked people what a winning culture, what winning behaviours look like, everyone could tell us, but almost no one does it. Winning and together. That's it.

Again, the cultural landing point is indisputable. As we sat around the board table in that premier league football club, we all knew what the aim was. Not many people thought it could be achieved, but everyone wanted to be part of trying.

There was a nuance in this landing point that is interesting and worth looking out for as you take your cultural change journey. If other cultural elements emerged during the change programme that were important to the stakeholders, that would be fine with the leadership team, as long as they supported the two critical components. Winning and together were explicitly the two most important things. That degree of clarity isn't always there, but when it is, it mustn't be ignored.

When combined, these first two elements form a powerful foundation upon which your cultural change programme can be built. They also provide a reference and evaluation point against which the success of the programme can be measured.

Create a clear, shared cultural narrative

We have already covered many of the key elements of a strong cultural narrative. Ideally in my view the narrative will be made up of a purpose, values and vision to give a rich sense of why people should engage with the organization, how it will be to be part of it and what the compelling future will look, sound and feel like.

The more people who are involved in the creation of the narrative, the better, providing that there is real and genuine commitment and connection to each element. Vitally, as you will see in the next chapter, the senior team must be 100 per cent committed to the process and the narrative that has been created.

By following these steps, you will have crossed the first of the chasms we identified during our cultural modelling project. Many of the organizations we explored didn't get to where they wanted to be, simply because they failed to define the strategic and cultural outcomes for the change programme. If you don't know where you are going, you will never get there.

The curse of underestimating scale

If you have followed this 'crossing the chasm' cultural change process so far, you and your colleagues will have done some considerable work, but it really is just the tip of the iceberg.

While each stage is crucial, and each chasm is terminal, the chasm that we call 'underestimating scale' is the one that we have seen the cultural change programmes of our clients and potential clients disappear down most often.

There is such a temptation, despite all best interests, to jump from the creation of the cultural narrative, to sharing it across the organization. This is mainly because those who have been part of creating it feel so connected to it that they assume everyone else will be too.

This underestimation of the scale of the work still to be done is a mistake that must be avoided at all costs, and you can avoid it by implementing the next two stages of our cultural change model.

Ensure the leadership team are fully committed and aligned

The thing that really makes cultural change hard is that people aren't stupid.

We saw the senior team walk out on stage together. This was the largest townhall meeting of their tour of the organization's hubs. They were sharing the latest business results, how the strategy would change in the year ahead and their joint commitment to change the culture to make it more collaborative and inclusive.

Each member of the executive team contributed to the section on results, each had their say on the strategic focus, but when it came to culture, the COO and hugely influential CFO remained silent.

Despite the energy and enthusiasm of the chief people officer and information systems director, who were very obviously the sponsors of, and drivers behind, the cultural shift, the programme pretty much died in that moment. The people knew that the senior team as a whole weren't serious about making the changes stick. Many of them had been around when the company changed the values. Nothing new happened then, nothing new will happen now.

Hedging and side-bet theory

We call this metaphorical – and in this example physical – stepping back, hedging. This cultural hedging involves people taking a step back in order to protect their reputation in case the new culture does not take a hold.

What they don't realize or acknowledge is the disastrous impact that their hedging has on the potential new culture. It is completely self-perpetuating. Because those involved don't want to be attached to a culture change programme that doesn't stick, they don't fully engage. Because they don't fully engage, the programme doesn't stick.

The opposite to cultural hedging is side-bet theory. Based on the work of Howard Becker in the 1960s, side-bet theory tells us that when every single executive is ready to risk their reputation on the new culture taking hold then this significantly increases the chances of the culture change programme delivering a successful outcome.

If you are a senior person involved in driving the culture change, here is what that means in practical terms. You and every single one of your senior colleagues becomes a sponsor of the new culture. You all actively promote the new culture but are also overt in your position that you are jointly and severally responsible for the success of the change programme. You must invite people throughout the organization to call you out the moment that they feel that you aren't setting the example culturally, or that they feel that something else is becoming more important.

This open invitation really does raise the stakes for each of you. Not only is the culture on the line now but your reputation is too. So many highly credible pieces of leadership research, including my favourite from Jim Kouzes and Barry Posner (2022), point to the fact that the number one characteristic that followers want from leaders is honesty, authenticity or congruence. We want leaders whose words and actions match up and who do what they say they are going to do. Perhaps even more importantly, these bodies of research tell us that if we make a commitment, like the cultural change outlined here, and we don't do everything we can collectively and individually to ensure that it is delivered, people lose belief in us. Not only do we damage how people see us in the context of culture, but their commitment to their work and engagement in the organization as a whole will be significantly reduced.

The willingness of the most senior team in the organization to bet their reputation individually and collectively on the success of a culture change programme is a huge step in securing the Alignment Advantage. It will set you aside from the degree of commitment demonstrated by most other senior teams.

Create a strategy to bring the culture to life

This section starts to demonstrate the brilliant logic of the ALIGNED® methodology. While so far we have distinguished strategy and culture as two separate elements, it also makes perfect sense to say that your cultural change programme is likely to form a strand of your business strategy.

Even if, for some reason, you decide to keep it completely separate, the process of building a rich, multi-faceted strategy to ensure that you deliver your cultural outcomes is a much more powerful process than the 'plan as you go' approach that is adopted in many culture change processes.

Vitally, it will force you as a team to take joint and several responsibility for the various outcomes and deliverables which will bring the culture to life.

It is worth reiterating the starting point for this section. Creating a strategy to bring the culture to life and ensuring the senior team are aligned and committed are two major steps to avoid underestimating the scale of work required. There is a danger of feeling like the creation of strategy is somehow slowing things down. After the excitement of having created the narrative, the natural sense is to want to do stuff, but without a solid strategic plan the risk is that you do the wrong things. My strong advice is to stick to the process.

Engaging the masses

We know 'the big bang launch' doesn't work. The new way of working is announced with an all-singing, all-dancing fanfare. The communication is clear but one-off. The energy and enthusiasm of one or two advocates fools nobody. The assumption that we can say to people 'Hey, this is important', and they will nod and make it important, is made time and time again.

There is a weird phenomenon that I observe regularly in the work that I do. People in organizations are willing to repeatedly do something that doesn't work because it is accepted as the norm, rather than trying a new and different approach that just might work. Engaging people in a new culture is a good example of this.

We know that as human beings we don't become engaged in or committed to something just because we are told that we should be. Yet, in the absence of knowing a better way, it is the approach that many leaders and organizations take.

Following the steps in this section will provide the antidote to this sure-fire point of failure in bringing your new culture to life. The steps require the most work and the most consistent and concerted effort throughout the organization, but by following them you will avoid the wall of resistance that comes when there is a lack of true engagement to the new culture.

The magic 20 per cent

Having said so clearly that big bang launches don't work, I want to give an equally clear alternative that will be immeasurably more successful.

Many years ago, a large financial services provider in the United Kingdom decided to create new ways of working, including new ways to measure and reward performance. They had tried countless times in the past to launch new reward and recognition systems, with each failing on the willingness of people at all levels of the organization to follow the process required to give the management community the data they required.

This time they decided to take a different approach. They selected small communities of people in different teams and departments to trial the approach. They were smart in who they selected. Typically, they were people who were in regular communication with a wide range of people in the business, and in many cases they were competitive characters who wanted to show that what they were doing was the best or most progressive. They also told those people involved in the trial that other people would know that they were part of the test group for the new system, but they weren't allowed to give others any detail about the new approach and why it was better.

In time this community become known as the fire starters. The change took hold successfully largely down to the fact that this group of people, who made up around 20 per cent of the total target audience, ignited interest in others. They went first, and because they were, others wanted to be on board too. They were connected enough to spread the word, engaged enough to be positive about the change, and competitive enough to want the change that they were early proponents of to be successful.

The approach that the human resources director took in this particular instance was a stroke of genius, but more importantly utilized three very significant and replicable principles that you should adopt too.

The law of diffusion of innovation

The law of diffusion of innovation was developed by Everett Rogers in 1962 and is one of the oldest social science theories that still stands true today. Rogers found that the adoption of a new product, behaviour or idea does not happen simultaneously in any community of people. Instead, we should see it as a process where some people are inclined to accept the change more readily.

Rogers identified five adopter categories who embrace the concept or idea at a different pace and when different needs are met.

1 **Innovators:** Innovators are interested in new ideas. They want to be involved at the outset, shaping the product or service. They are willing to take risks as they try the new thing out. In the context of culture change, these are the people who will ideally be involved in shaping the narrative. At a minimum, these will be the first group of fire starters around which the rest of the change

community will be built. Innovators will make up around 2.5 per cent of any typical community.

2 **Early adopters:** These are what we would class as influencers in the modern social media world. Early adopters have a consistent sense of the need to change and evolve, and so they want to be at the forefront of trying new ideas and products. Like innovators, early adopters will put their own reputation on the line to demonstrate and advocate new approaches and behaviours, which makes them vital in our culture change programmes. In most cases this group will be connected and have influence within a particular network. Early adopters will make up around 13.5 per cent of any typical community.

3 **Early majority:** In short, the early majority won't try something until someone else has tried it with some degree of success. My experience would categorize these people as sceptics rather than cynics that will never fully adopt a new way of working just because they were told it was a good idea. The early majority will make up around 34 per cent of any typical community.

4 **Late majority:** It is not unfair in my experience to assume that those in the late majority are sceptical of most change. They will only adopt a new product, idea or in this case culture after they see that it has overtly been adopted by the majority of their peers and that it is very definitely here to stay. I would also suggest that while some of the late majority are long-time products of their environment or perhaps their personality, there are some people who find a home here as a result of seeing so many new initiatives fade and fail. When we manage to engage these people, we can be sure that the fire of our new culture is well and truly lit. The late majority will make up around 34 per cent of any typical community.

5 **Laggards:** Laggards are so intertwined with, and connected to, 'the way we have always done things around here' that they are almost impossible to truly engage in an approach. They are typically risk averse and will hold on to traditions 'just because'. In the context of cultural change, it is rarely of any real benefit to

invest significant time and energy in bringing laggards on the journey. They will invariably find an argument not to be part of the change process. Instead, I advise focusing on the other four categories and ensuring that the new culture comes to life with the vast majority of the organization. At that stage the laggards become the outliers and have a simple choice to engage or to find a new organization that is more aligned with their mindset. Laggards will make up around 16 per cent of any typical community.

The majority of people in your organization won't adopt a new way of being, until they see others doing it first. By building a community of around 20 per cent of people who will create, develop, embrace and champion the culture first, you create a watershed beyond which the masses will engage in new behaviours, activities and approaches.

Scarcity and social proof

Dr Robert Cialdini has been researching, educating on and writing about influence and persuasion since the early 1980s. He is best known for his six principles of influence, which he covers in brilliant practical detail in his 1984 book *Influence: The psychology of persuasion* and, from 2008, *Yes! 50 scientifically proven ways to be persuasive*.

All six principles have their place in the process of developing and bringing to life a new culture, but two in particular, scarcity and social proof, integrate beautifully into the law of diffusion of innovation.

How the magic 20 per cent creates scarcity

In recent years, the principle of scarcity has become more commonly known as FOMO – the fear of missing out. We have an automatic response, or to use Cialdini's term, a 'click whir', to want what we can't have. Marketeers and sales people use this regularly to entice people to 'buy now'. Many airlines will show you on their website how many seats are left to buy at the existing price, while Amazon will show you that there are only a few of the product that you're browsing left in stock. Even though our logic will tell us that if anyone can replenish their stock quickly, Amazon can, we are still more likely to buy because of the scarcity of the product and our fear of missing out.

This helps to explain why the magic 20 per cent of people who are involved in your culture change programme are so important in engaging the masses. As this combination of innovators and early adopters demonstrate their involvement and engagement in the new way of being, it creates a sense of scarcity or fear of missing out, especially in your early majority. People will start to want to be part of the new culture simply because they aren't.

How the magic 20 per cent creates social proof

Cialdini's principle of social proof is built on the 'click whir' that we want to have or do what others have or do. We are more likely to do what others do, and even more likely to do what others that we like or are like do.

This is demonstrated brilliantly in an experiment that Cialdini shares in *Yes! 50 scientifically proven ways to be persuasive.*

Anyone who has ever stayed in a hotel will have seen some kind of sign in the bathroom inviting them to re-use their towels more than once. The signs that you will have typically seen are likely to say something like, 'We are committed to protecting the environment. If you would like to help us in that commitment, please consider using your towels more than once.' In the experiment, the signs were reworded to say '75 per cent of our guests re-use their towels at some time during their stay, so please do so as well.' The result was a 26 per cent increase in towel re-use. Guests were shown proof that others were re-using their towels, and this social proof influenced their behaviour to do the same.

The experiment did not stop there. Imagine the next time you stay in a hotel, in the bathroom there was a sign that said: '75 per cent of people who have stayed in this room used their towel more than once.' Well, based on Cialdini's experience this small additional change in language, to make the social proof more specific led to a 33 per cent increase in re-use.

If you contrast this use of social proof in the process of bringing alive a new culture, with the traditional big bang launch, we can quickly see why one is infinitely more successful than the other. Launches that say, 'Hey, do this, because we the bosses say so' provide no social proof. When we enlist a small community of fire starters who can demonstrate that the culture is already alive and that their colleagues – the people who are like them – are already living it, it is inevitable that other people will jump on board too.

Develop and mobilize cross-level, cross-discipline change teams

So far, we have explored the theories, models and science behind the 'engaging the masses' part of the crossing the chasm culture change process. Now we can move on to how you practically utilize these tools. The first step is to develop and mobilize cross-level and cross-discipline change teams.

The specific projects will come a little later, but during our exploration of organizations that had made culture change programmes stick, one very obvious element that I would not necessarily have expected was the investment that the organizations made in the development of those who were playing a key role in the change. There is a subtle but important difference between throwing a team together and asking them to work out how we can do some things differently, and bringing those people together and giving them some very specific development.

The scale of development will shift depending on the size of your organization, the budget available to develop your people, and the solidity of the business case you laid out at the beginning of the process, but ideally your culture change champions will be developed in the following areas:

- What is the new cultural narrative; how do they connect with it; what are their stories that bring the narrative to life? In particular they must be crystal clear about how what they do connects to the purpose, how their personal values connect to the new organizational values and how they will contribute to the new vision being realized. They should also see the importance of others having these connections.

- What makes a high-performing team, whether this is a temporary project team or a permanent work team? This foundational understanding will help to minimize political challenges that often crop up when working with cross-functional colleagues.

- What is the psychology of change and how do they bring others on a change journey? This might be as simple as sharing overtly the change process that they are part of, including crossing the chasm, the law of diffusion of innovation, and Dr Cialdini's principles of influence. Ideally, if you have the facilitation skills available, you would help the champions develop their own principles and tools for engaging their colleagues in the journey.

There is a plethora of other development that these people are likely to benefit from, including leadership, managing upwards, presence and credibility, coaching and even project management, but these aren't always necessary, while the three areas above are foundational to the magic 20 per cent really making a difference.

As well as creating a group of highly engaged, highly motivated and well-skilled change facilitators, you are covertly creating even more of a sense of scarcity and fear of missing out among those who are not part of the process.

These facilitators will lead on the change programmes that will really bring the culture to life. With the support of the senior leadership to model the way that demonstrates the importance of making meaningful change, they will become the glue that really makes the new culture stick.

The importance of this community being cross-level and cross-discipline must not be overlooked. Culture change is not top down or bottom up, it is from the inside out. Frontline people are vital as they really know what is needed to ensure that the real face of the organization connects with the change. Senior people are vital as we need people in change teams that have the authority to make decisions, access budget and hold senior colleagues' hands to the flame. We need technical specialists working closely with operational co-workers, collaborating, developing, driving, delivering and demonstrating that we really are all in this together and no part of the organization will be able to avoid being part of this new way of being.

If you are driving culture change within a specific team, the cross-functional element may be less relevant. It is important to consider how you can make your magic 20 per cent as diverse as possible. If you can get a cross-section of your team that would never usually work closely on a specific project working together and on the same page, this will send out a very powerful message.

You should consider your role as the most senior person in the team very carefully. In some cases, if you have a very empowered team, and if you are very good at not making decisions for them, it may be beneficial for you to be part of the change team. You may decide that you shouldn't be part of it, but that you will create some clear ground rules as to when they can, or should, involve you as a trusted advisor, or the ultimate decision-maker. Or you may decide to remain as distant from the magic 20 per cent as possible. While you and your team members might find this challenging, it is particularly important if the culture change is to become more empowered and self-sufficient, and for them to be able to think for themselves more.

There is not a single right answer to this conundrum, but it is a decision you must make early in the process.

Initiate multiple business projects with slightly unrealistic timescales

Pace is a powerful tool when it comes to culture change. 'Slow and steady' sends a message that this isn't important. Make changes slightly quicker than people find palatable.

One of the first serious culture change programmes that I supported was with a purpose-led third sector organization that cared deeply for its people and end users. They were reorganizing, restructuring and changing the culture in order to be able to meet their service users' needs in the face of government-imposed budget cuts. In short, they had to be more commercial.

They cared so deeply for their people that they took considerable time over every element of the change, doing everything they could to dot every 'i' and cross every 't'. A reorganization of the 1,500-person workforce took nearly three years, and throughout the fear of change and a perceived threat of redundancy lingered and grew into a toxic and negative barrier to performance. The reason the pace was so slow was to ensure their people were OK. However, the sedentary pace had exactly the opposite effect. By the end of the process, only three people faced redundancy, yet many more skilled and previously committed people bailed out of the organization in the following months, unable to move on the from elongated change process.

In culture change, being a little too quick is always better than being a little too slow.

This in itself may not seem like a radical idea, but married with the need to initiate multiple business projects, imposing challenging time-lines is likely to create a degree of frisson. And, to a certain degree, this is exactly what is required at this stage of the change process.

The change projects will be designed to anchor the culture in the day-to-day workings of the organization. This is a point that is missed so often in culture change programmes. As I have pointed to in previous chapters, culture is more than how we act with each other. To really make culture change stick, it must be interwoven into the very fabric of the work that the organization does. If you are leading culture change in your organization, you must ensure that every process, policy and procedure is reflective of the culture you want to bring to life.

The very obvious place to start is with processes that most directly influence your people. Your values must be present in your recruitment, your performance management, and in absence, parental leave and all other HR policies. It is difficult to have an organization value like 'we care' and also have restrictive policies that force new parents back to work after the minimum statutory leave.

Equally, if we accept that our organization's values should be reflective of the most commonly shared values of its people, then it also makes sense that we should ensure that we are recruiting people whose personal values overlap with those organizational values. If this means revising our recruitment process to include this assessment, then this should be one of the early projects.

Performance management is another area that is usually owned by HR departments, and it is so important in the culture change process that I have dedicated the following chapter to the topic. Human resources policies and procedures are an easy target for cultural integration and do produce great results; however, they should be the tip of the iceberg. Every part of the organization must review their workings and logistics and make changes to make them more reflective of the culture. In two decades of partnering with, and providing services to, organizations across the world, I have only ever received one welcome letter from a procurement team. Having been through a comprehensive, but very user-friendly, approval process, the short letter arrived welcoming us to their supplier list, accompanied by some contact details in the unlikely event of any issues with invoices or payments. If you have never been on this side of the procurement process, that is a very different experience compared to the majority of organizations. So much so that I called the contact who had signed the letter to find out why they had done so. The reply was simple, 'Because our values tell us that this is the right thing for us to do.'

When I have shared this anecdote with people in other organizations, they often respond by saying, if the procurement lives the values, then everyone must. While I wouldn't go so far as to generalize about procurement procedures and the people who create them, it certainly is an example of an organization that had clearly made sure that their values, and therefore their culture, was alive in every part of the business.

Even with a highly motivated and cross-functional team of change champions, you aren't going to be able tackle every policy, process and procedure in one go. Here are six questions to help you decide which to tackle first:

1 What policy or process will most obviously show that the new culture is here to stay if we change it?

2 What policy or process will be the easiest to change?

3 What policy or process needs to be changed anyway, with the new culture just becoming another factor in the change process?

4 Which policy, process or procedure would have the biggest impact on the customer when changed?

5 What processes will have the most impact on business if they are changed to reflect the new culture?

6 What would the culture champions love to change first?

My experience is that there isn't a single correct answer to which policies, processes and procedures should be tackled in the first round of change projects; however, by answering these questions it is likely to be emergent which will have the biggest impact.

Whichever are tackled first, the timeline for completion of the change must be tight. If it is a case of rewriting a procedure, it should be changed, tested and implemented within 30 days. A larger change, that perhaps has an impact on a large number of people, should still be driven through in 60 to 90 days. Even a large-scale system change should be tackled with a 90- to 120-day timeline. In some organizations this may seem aspirational, but that is the point. You must drive culture change in a way that demonstrates its importance strategically and on your customers' experience.

One final note on cross-functional change teams who drive change projects with tight deadlines – the success of this part of the change process rests on the maintenance of momentum. The moment it looks like the momentum is dropping or wavering, it must be stepped up again. Even if it feels somewhat unrelenting for a period of a few months, this work will inject the new culture into every part of the organization. The more powerful that injection is, the stronger and longer lasting it will be.

Getting to the cultural landing point

In our original piece of work modelling organizations that had unsuccessfully tried to change their culture, some of the most surprising findings came towards the end of their culture change journey.

We found some organizations had done so much good work, including the integration of the new culture into some of their working practices, yet it still faded and lost its way. When we examined what these organizations had done in comparison to those that reached the cultural landing point, with the culture they set out to create being 'the way they be around here', those that didn't quite hit the mark neglected three small but significant steps.

1. Make the new ways of working your standard working practices

If led well, your projects will gain and drive a great deal of energy. People will be excited and challenged enough to develop new ways of working. It is easy, though, to neglect the need to nail this new culturally aligned process, policies and procedures.

As unsexy a step in the process as it might be, it is so important to do everything you can to ensure that the new way becomes the only way. This includes the update of everything from intranet systems to interview documents, from induction training to the forms that go out to your clients, customers, visitors or guests.

The challenge of not doing this is that the new approaches don't stick. They are perceived, sometimes unconsciously, as a fad. In one organization we observed a puzzling trend. Those who had been in the organization longer were adopting new cultural practices better than those who had joined the organization since the new culture had been adopted.

It was only with some subtle detective work that we uncovered that the people who were new to the organization were being trained on, and guided by, old policies and processes. There had been some simple but significant oversights in updating some standard working practices. This meant that while existing people were blazing a trail in bringing the new culture to life, new colleagues, many of whom had been sold the new culture during their recruitment process, were learning and implementing the old ways of working.

2. Ensure all development activities underpin the new ways of working

While there is a significant overlap to the previous point, ensuring that development activities underpin and support the new culture is more than just updating the training materials.

You must ensure that the way you develop your people reflects the culture. If your culture suggests that you are creative or innovative in the way you operate, the traditional 'pour and snore' approach to learning just won't do.

If your culture points to agility, leanness and making every pound, dollar and euro count, then again, your approach to developing your people should reflect this.

The focus and activities of any type of development materials must also be reflective of the culture.

Learning is not about the consumption of information, instead it is about the creation of value, meaning, belief and action.

In any organization where culture is important, unless that culture is for them to do as they are told and conform without question, the development activities must help people to understand what is important to them about what they are learning, why it is important in their context, and it must then develop the skills and behaviours required. Far too much training and development in the corporate world – and beyond – focuses on what we should do and why we should do it, without really connecting the development or our beliefs and values as a human being.

Those organizations who create ALIGNED® approaches to learning can be sure that development activities will have significantly more impact than those that don't.

3. Review the project and celebrate success

The final stage of our 'crossing the chasm' culture change framework came from perhaps the most surprising observation from our modelling work. When we noticed the pattern it was obvious, but without the insight from the companies that we learned from I certainly would not have included it in a framework and process like this.

There were some organizations who followed a culture change process that was solid and systematic. It included many of the elements that I have laid out in this chapter, and their new culture began to take hold. Yet, in the weeks and months beyond the main culture change activities, it began to drift. In some cases it reverted, not completely, back to the previous culture but certainly there was a significant regression. In others, it morphed into something else. In the same way that a virus mutates, there was a definite deviation from the culture that the incumbents had set out to create.

Upon examination, a clear pattern emerged. Those organizations that celebrated their new culture, who made a clear demarcation that said 'This is where we were, this is where we are now' further embedded that culture into the hearts and minds of their people. The organizations that didn't clearly signify and signpost the change ran a clear risk that the culture would drift. It didn't apply to every single organization, but certainly a high enough percentage for me to say clearly that the final stage of our culture change framework was to cement the culture by celebrating the journey and outcome publicly.

All those involved in the early stages of the programme should be recognized for their contribution. Evidence of the new cultural chapter should be shared, and the journey that every area of the organization has been on should be marked. Not only does this celebration acknowledge the work of everyone involved, but it clearly anchors the new culture as 'the way we be around here'.

Maintaining cultural consistency

The phrase 'we used to, but we stopped', is the enemy of powerful cultures. The only way to maintain a culture that contributes to your organization grabbing the Alignment Advantage is to be ruthless in your consistent monitoring and leadership of it.

Operational crises will come and go. Stakeholder demands will ebb and flow, and those for whom you create your X will require urgent attention. But as long as we agree and acknowledge that our organization's culture is the vital pivot between our strategy and the brand and experience that we create for our customers, then we must be unwavering in our work to keep it at the top of every agenda. Not because it's a nice thing to do, but because it is a strategic imperative.

Reference

Cialdini, R B (1984) *Influence: The psychology of persuasion*, HarperCollins, New York

Goldstein, N J, Martin, S J and Cialdini, R B (2008) *Yes! 50 scientifically proven ways to be persuasive*, Free Press, New York

Kouzes, J and Posner, B (2022) *The Leadership Challenge*, 7th edn, Jossey-Bass, New York

08

ALIGNED® performance management

In the previous chapter, I acknowledged the vital importance of integrating your culture into your performance management system. For many clients, this process seems unnecessarily difficult. In fact, our experience tells us that performance management approaches often look to combat ineffectiveness by increasing the complexity of the whole process. Taking an ALIGNED® approach combats that by focusing on three specific functional areas to ensure that we are getting a useful picture about the contribution that the individuals in our organization are making.

At this point I want to acknowledge the work of Brian Lumsdon in creating this framework. Brian was the first person to join TwentyOne Leadership around six months after Joanne and I had founded it. He made a profound contribution to the business and remains a close partner to this day.

Performance measures

The fundamental reason that we monitor and measure performance in the first place is to ensure that our people are doing the job that they are being paid to do. It is also fair to acknowledge that our people want to know that they are contributing in the right way to the success of the organization. For these combined reasons, we should create a set of performance measures that tell you as my manager, and me as your direct report, what me doing a good job looks like. Whether the measures are in the form of empirical targets, smart objectives or competencies, the most important thing is that we are able to assess clearly whether I have done what I needed to do.

I want to pause at this point. So many performance management systems obsess about the complexities of the process, but at the heart of performance management is what you have just read. I need to know what I need to do to do a good job, and you as my manager need to know if I have done that. Everything else must be in service of that.

If I were to delve into the relative complexities of where the objectives are formed, I would urge you to keep three things in mind.

The first is that all performance measures should be connected to part of the strategy. If people are collectively doing work that helps to deliver the strategy then the strategy is likely to be achieved. This is another element of the Alignment Advantage which is obvious when stated, but I am certain that you have been in jobs where your performance measures had no obvious connection to the strategy. If the management community don't know the strategy well enough to be able to create measures that connect to it, it is an issue with the communication and understanding of the strategy rather than with performance measurement. Hopefully this isn't a challenge in your organization, and you can confidently say that your own performance measures connect directly to the strategy.

This leads me to my second point in creating effective measures of performance. If your performance measures are strategy-based it makes perfect sense for your people's measures to be a chunked-down version of your own deliverables. In that way you can be sure that you are delegating the right deliverables at the right level to the right people. There will be some things for which you, as the manager, must be accountable and responsible for delivering, but fundamentally your people's performance measures should be a division of your own.

My third point is a watch-out. If my key performance measures are what helps you decide whether I am doing a decent job or not then, by nature, it should be fully within my influence whether I deliver on them or not. The goals become much more unhelpful and the conversations much more uncomfortable when some of the goals aren't in my control, for example, a host in a car dealership who has the overall customer satisfaction of the dealership as one of their objectives, or the salesperson who has the collective target for the department in their performance measures. This is a simple error that reduces the value of your performance measurement systems to virtually zero. Ensure that what you are asking your people to deliver, they can. This is a simple point but an important one.

Stretch measures

One fundamental challenge with most performance measurement systems is that they help us to measure and deliver a thoroughly average job. If we want our people to feel stretched and developed, if we want to understand more clearly who our future successors are, and if we want to continue to raise the performance bar, then we should introduce some stretch measures into our performance system.

These measures will be things that our people can strive to achieve, but if they don't manage to they are not underperforming. In fact, in many cases, the attitude with which they attempt the stretch goals is as important as the achievement of them. Stretch measures can take the form of a range of goals or objectives and should be aspirational and stretching, rather than impossible to achieve, given the individual's skill level and sphere of influence.

Cultural measures

I have believed for a long time, and still do now, that the hardest problem for most managers to deal with is the high performer who has the wrong attitude. One of the most-read articles that I have ever written is entitled 'Why a brilliant jerk will ruin your team'. High-performing or experienced people who are culturally misaligned are hugely damaging if not challenged. Not only do they chip away at your whole culture with their actions and behaviours, but they also give other people permission to do the same. Perhaps worst of all, if left unchecked, they provide a cue to the people with the right attitudes and behaviours that it is time to leave. Over time you lose more of your good people, giving more of the power to those who don't act in the right way, and inevitably your culture shifts for the worse.

While this can be a complex challenge, the antidote is relatively simple. As a leader you must include a cultural measure in your performance measurement process. This could be as simple as creating an additional objective that says something along the lines of 'and you do all of the above in line with the organization's values'. Even the introduction of this most simple of measures allows you to manage those people who get the job done but in a culturally misaligned way. More positively, it provides a platform for those who are culturally aligned to share examples of when and how they have lived and breathed the culture.

Your cultural measure can be more complex, with specific performance measures linked to specific elements of your cultural narrative, but the outcome must remain in focus. Do these cultural measures allow those people who do live and breathe the culture in everything that they do to demonstrate that this is the case, and do they allow you as the manager to manage those that are culturally and attitudinally misaligned?

Bringing ALIGNED® performance measurement together

Imagine I worked for you in a learning and development role. I believe it is possible for you to manage my performance in an aligned way via five to six well-crafted objectives. The first three to four would be my performance objectives. They would be the meat and drink of what I need to deliver over the next quarter. The objectives will be SMART, aligned with your objectives and aligned with the strategic objectives of our department and, ultimately, the organization. There will be an additional stretch objective. You have lifted this directly from your objectives. You don't expect me to deliver it fully, but want me to create a plan as if I was going to. I am excited by the opportunity to do something that sits a little outside of my regular work. Finally, I have an objective that reminds me to do all of these things in line with the company purpose, values and vision. It is clear, uncomplicated and practical for us both.

ALIGNED® performance measurement is a great way to bring the Alignment Advantage to life for everyone in your organization. Perhaps more importantly, though, it is a process that counteracts the cumbersome ineffective performance systems that are the bane of the lives of so many managers.

INTERVIEW Strategy and marketing
Sue Bridgewater

Professor Sue Bridgewater is passionate about helping people to achieve their potential and making education accessible. She is an experienced educator with extensive experience in the fields of business, management and sport.

She has designed, led and delivered leadership education across undergraduate, postgraduate and executive education levels to clients including Philips, Nestlé, HSBC, KPMG, IBM, Ford, Diageo and Prudential while also directing the Centre for Sports Business at University of Liverpool Management School, which is a Centre of Excellence in research and teaching in the field of business of sport and football.

Her reach in the industry of professional football is as impressive as it is broad. Sue has directed the League Managers' Association Diploma Programme for professional football managers for over 20 years and she is a Director of Women in Football, working to support, champion, mentor and create equal opportunities for women in football.

This interview demonstrates why I rate Sue as one of the very best minds on marketing that I have had the pleasure of working with. She shares her insights on strategy initially then focuses on what separates great marketing and great marketers from the rest.

How would you define strategy?
There are so many descriptions and definitions of strategy, but I always come back to it having a number of different components. One of them is, it has to be about direction. It is the big goal that the company or organization has to achieve. Next is the plan of action to get to that goal. The third element is the resources. The strategy makes clear how to mobilize the

resources and capabilities of that organization to achieve the goals. The different elements are what makes it difficult to give a single definition.

One way to capture the different aspects of strategy in a definition is to align with Mintzberg's 5Ps of strategy:

- They start with the plan, which represents the direction towards the end goal.

- The next is the ploy. It isn't my favourite word but it represents game theory or at least the decisions you will make relative to your competition's position. What are you trying to provoke? Will you undercut them or charge a premium?

- Pattern acknowledges and suggests that there are occasions where strategy is emergent, and in other cases the whole approach is completely deliberate.

- Next is the position. This represents the market and your understanding of what your customers want.

- Perspective focuses on the viewpoint of the individuals in the organization.

There are a lot of elements to Mintzberg's framework but that's why I like it. It reinforces that there is a lot to a 'proper' strategy.

This also highlights that creating a strategy is a complex piece of work, so what do you see as the advantage of investing the time and energy in creating a proper strategy rather than working from a simple business plan?
Fundamentally, strategy creates clarity. Sometimes it is hard to narrow down the collective thinking and action in the organization to a precise set of strategy objectives, but it is important for clarity. It is possible to create a plan that ignores the interactions and tensions in, for example, increasing market share or increasing profit.

Good strategic processes also promote a quality of thought that can be missing in organizations that are light on strategy. So many people jump straight into the detail of launching a product, or get straight into action, without really being clear about what the big picture and strategic goals they are trying to achieve are. I think strategy is very important to force them to stand back or stand above.

We refer to this as threshold learning. Once you know the strategic process, you can't un-know it, and it changes the way you think about business and how organizations work. This makes the process of strategic thought more important than the various tools and concepts that can be used. It almost doesn't matter which tools you're using as long as it helps you to take a strategic standpoint above it. I think it is very important for organizations to understand the world that they're in and try to agree on where it is they're trying to get to.

When you work with students, business leaders or those in sporting environments, what are the key insights and most important learnings as they explore strategy?

I quite often come back to the Drucker triangle, in which the three elements are the environment, the market and the organization. In my view the power of the model is not the three elements in isolation, but in how they interact. The context to me is that the world and our business environment are changing fast, and change is just getting faster. Change was once much more gradual. We were much more able to use things that analysed historic data to try to predict what was going to happen in the future. Now there is much more discontinuous change to add into the context that organizations function in.

Big disruptions to markets that change things completely are much more the norm, so we have to acknowledge this in the assumptions that we make. I was reading something recently that suggested we are operating in the world of economics of shortage. Can we assume now that we can actually source things from India or China? Can we be sure that we are going to be able to get the chips or the paracetamol or whatever it is and just move it around the world? We wouldn't have thought that a few years ago, but the Covid-19 pandemic has changed the environment. So strategically, when we set goals we have to think about context, resources, environment, capability and how we can mobilize to cover the gaps. We have to think of the strategic in the context of a fast-moving market. There must be a permanent process in the strategy of reviewing and revisiting.

If this is a five-year strategy, you aren't going to go through the whole process of achieving it and never change it. What happens if you massively overachieve? If you have exceeded the goal in year one. What will you do? Or what if the world has changed? You need to go back and revisit it. So the fit between your strategy and your environment, your context, is really important. Remember the third element of the Drucker triangle is the organization. The organizations that are successful are the ones that can adapt, that can keep on looking at all the elements and realize that they need to change their strategies. The very best pre-empt, maybe, some of the things that are going to happen and shift accordingly. They have the ability, not just to look at historic data, but to think about scenarios and possibilities, and shifting to make the most of them, or to do the kind of things they should be doing. The best organizations strategically keep ahead in their thinking about the market, the environment and the shape of their businesses.

How do you respond when someone says that their organization is moving too fast to have a strategy?

One of the examples I've used for years is a company that I used to work with that was part of a big multinational textiles business. Part of the business was called Dynacast. They used to make all the little metal spools that the thread went round. They were precision castings for a specific market. As the textiles market and environment changed, the parent company and many of its parts were struggling, but Dynacast shifted their focus and used their skills in other areas like mobile telephony, laptops and automotive. The market changed, the environment changed, and they responded.

Your strategy has to flex, but it gives you the guide point from which to flex.

You have worked with some organizations that are the best at marketing in the world and lots that aren't so good. What separates the best from the rest?

When I stand back and look at an organization's approach to marketing, whether it's a big multinational or a sporting organization, it always seems to me that it is not so much what they do as how they do it. When I teach somebody about marketing and they understand the basics of it, the models, the frameworks, the response is very often 'Well, obviously.' Saying we should understand what the customers value is obvious. We should know what they need and want – well yes, of course I'm going to analyse the data to try to find that out, it is just a sensible thing to do. It all sounds like it's going to be easy.

Students and organizations start the process and very quickly find that it is not in fact that easy. Finding the right data isn't always easy. If you find it, analysing that data to actually gain useful insights isn't that easy. Having the innovative, creative ideas that will allow you to capture value more than your competitors isn't straightforward. Even when you've done all of that, you have to engage with your customers, make sure that you're delivering value but also communicating value. So I think the organizations that are doing it better than anybody else are doing the fundamentals well and in a way that works for them. It's not just what they are doing, but how they are doing it.

The best organizations have their marketing strategy and day-to-day, hour-to-hour, they are actually understanding their markets better. They get the right data. They get valuable insights from that data that maybe other people aren't spotting. They are being innovative and creative. They are prepared to disrupt, but disrupt based on a strategy and on data and insight.

Another difference is that they really market from a customer's viewpoint. Many organizations say they do this, but it is much less common than marketers would like to admit. The best engage with, and interact with, customers in a way that really communicates their value to their customers.

So it seems that in some organizations there is a gap between the data they have and the marketing insight they gain from it?
Absolutely. I think we've all got a bit obsessed with this idea that data is king. You could have all of this data and assume that just having the data is somehow giving you this big advantage, but what are you going to do with it? It's both what data you have and what you do with it. The obvious organization for nailing both sides of that is Amazon, and so my comment on all of marketing is really, how do you put all the pieces together in a way that gives you some kind of advantage and that shows that you are offering more value or a different type of value? How do you use all the tools to do it in a way that customers are going to identify with and see that you have got something that other people haven't got?

Where does brand fit into the whole marketing ecosystem?
Brand, too, is of course really important. I have taught about brand for many years, and I still find it quite interesting that in some models of marketing brand doesn't get a separate heading. Sometimes brand is positioned more like an implementation tool, but brand is really the way we capture value. It's almost like a shorthand. It's a way to get the customer to know that if you see that thing, you have an understanding of what value you're going to get from that company. A brand, in some ways, is a bundle of value. Let's take McDonald's. I might not necessarily be a big fan of McDonald's, but if I see a McDonald's logo, I know what value I'm going to get.

If you look at the fundamentals of a marketing model like Kotler and Keller, they put the two sides together. This is what the marketers are trying to do, and this is what the customers are trying to get. There are the various ways in which you're capturing the value from the company, the personality of the brand, the physical aspects like the Coca-Cola bottle or the Louboutin red-soled shoes. Then you have the customer thinking, does that reflect a set of values that I want to associate myself with? Therefore, do I want a relationship with them?

I think branding is so important because it's the bridge between, in some of the strategy work, all of those resources and capabilities and things that the organization could do or could offer, and how you then turn that into something that you are going to communicate and deliver to the customers in a way they value.

Where does customer insight fit into all of that?
When I reflect back to learning about marketing in the 1980s and how it developed in the 1990s, the customer was king, and the market analysis was the first part of any module on marketing. The timeline was always market analysis, marketing strategy, implementation, planning and control. We would say that you have to understand the customers and what they value before you can actually develop the aspects of the brand. That way you would know that the target customer was going to value it. It feels very much like that viewpoint has shifted to a belief that we can build relationships with customers so they value what we offer. There is more interaction in this digital area throughout the journey so customer insight upfront isn't given the same value, but I believe it still should be.

We should still start off with customer insight, but also be using customer insight at every point in that. So if you actually launch into the market and your website is getting feedback from customers that there's some things they are not happy with, we can compare to the original insight and decide whether we need to go back to the drawing board altogether or tweak part of the offering.

Even in the new world that includes such just-in-time digital marketing and feedback, I still see customer insight as a core tenet of a marketing strategy. As in so many areas of work and life, so much changes, but certain vital elements of marketing remain the same. I reinforce this to students on our programmes every year. Every generation, every time there is a significant change in the market, people think that it is a whole new world. There will be changes and updates, but the fundamentals of good marketing haven't changed as much as some people would want us to think. Remember when the internet came along, and people said it was going to kill TV and radio marketing. Of course it has radically shifted the dial, but TV and radio advertising are still going strong, albeit with different parameters. We have more channels, more ways to execute our strategy, and a good marketing strategy, supported by the right customer insight, will shape which of these we exploit. Digital will invariably be part of these strategies, but digital marketing isn't a separate thing; it is another tool in our strategic marketing toolkit.

If you were to identify the single most important piece of marketing research or insight that everyone should know, what would it be?
That is a really hard one because I think there is more than one. Certainly one would be Keller's customer-based brand equity (CBBE) model because I probably use that more than I use anything else. Originally focused on museums, the approach emphasizes that you have to understand what the customers see as value and then understand how you build a brand relationship with them. This and Kotler and Keller's work are two of the key things in terms of understanding the balance between the value you have created as an organization and what the customer sees as value.

I read a great piece in *Harvard Business Review* recently called 'Why marketing analytics hasn't lived up to its promise' by Carl F Mela and Christine Moorman. It's based on a 2018 article and reinforces that you have to get the right data and integrate it. You have to get insight out of your data to ensure value creation. It is a really nicely written piece.

Again, I say this to students regularly, so much focus is on marketing tactics and implementation, but we have to use the data and the insights from it to inform those tactics. It is too easy to make assumptions based on our preferences.

We are back to the original classic point that the customer is king. You have to look at marketing and brand through the customer's eyes. There is a tendency to be swept along by the newest technology or the latest case study or the latest social media guru and miss what the data tells us we should do to demonstrate what our customers value.

How do you see the culture of an organization influencing the perceptions of its customers?

The connection has been made for many decades. If you look at the brand iceberg model, it highlights that the brand is the bit that you see above the surface, but it's a small proportion of your iceberg. There are lots more elements below the surface and that includes the organization's values, and we know that values shape or represent the culture. The argument is that unless you are living internally, whatever it is that you are trying to get the customers to experience, it isn't going to be authentic. In turn, you won't be able to deliver the brand promise on a day-to-day basis.

One organization took the view that everyone needed to understand what we were looking to deliver. Not just the people in the retail store or in customer service positions, but the people in your gatehouse and the people in your factory need to understand it. They believed that only then would they be consistent in how they deliver and communicate value to the customer. The danger of not taking that view is that you can do things in one part of the business, and spend a lot of money on achieving what you need to, yet other parts of the business can actually be doing the opposite.

This points to the same thing as you do. Culture and brand must be lined up and both should be present in the overall strategy of the business. The insight that we gain from our customers should be baked into the strategic intent of the business. It shouldn't be an afterthought. It shouldn't be a sideline. It goes back to the original point about the customer is king; we know that organizations that see this from a strategic perspective are going to be more successful in the long term.

In her interview Professor Bridgewater makes two vital and somewhat unfashionable points. The first relates to the importance of data and measuring what is important. This links perfectly to ALIGNED® performance measurement. I believe that the view that what gets measured gets delivered is never outdated. The other point is that while new models, approaches and developments will add to our armoury, we shouldn't overlook the value of good, longstanding approaches that stand the test of time. I would posit that this also applies perfectly to great performance management.

09

What is the X and why?

As the ALIGNED® methodology developed over the years, and what we now call the Alignment Advantage became clear, the X had several iterations and focuses. For a time we focused, almost solely, on the customers' buying or service experiences, but all too often questions about brand and reputation, and when the customers' journey actually began, challenged my thinking about customer experience.

For a time we focused on brand, and all that comes with understanding what brand really is and what it stands for. We worked on the basis that brand and customer experience are indistinguishable. This was a useful position for a while, but it soon became clear that customer experience and brand are two different sides of the same coin. They have so much in common, but they aren't the same thing. They have some unique inputs and drivers, and they certainly require different measures.

In time, as we worked with more organizations using the ALIGNED® methodology, and as we examined and modelled many more, we realized that when an organization's thinking and action appertaining to brand and customer experience are fully aligned, then their customers, guests, visitors or clients feel an X-factor. In that moment the X was born.

The X is the combination of brand in its truest sense, and customer experience in its most complete form.

More on the service/experience distinction

I once had a meeting with the head of customer experience for one of the big four UK supermarkets. We chatted informally about all things customer. She was talented, charismatic and open. She told me about various customer initiatives they had put in place, including the engagement of, at great expense, a new agency to carry out all of their in-store mystery shopping.

After a while I asked the experience question: if I was to come into one of your stores, what would be the experience that you would want me to have that would be distinct from your competitors? After some considerable contemplation, she confessed that she had never considered that question before. I asked her how she knew what she wanted the mystery shoppers to assess. The truth was the experience that her customers had was going to be decided by the mystery shopping partner, not by those in the organization.

What was clear from our further conversations was that they knew about their customers and their shopping habits, but they knew virtually nothing about the experiences their customers wanted to have while they were shopping. And because of this they had no way of distinguishing themselves from their closest competitors other than on price.

An experience mindset allows a distinction beyond but including product and price. There is a reason that the likes of Waitrose and Aldi have thrived outside of the traditional big four UK supermarkets. They have a clear, distinct experience.

As I highlighted in the early chapters, employee experience (EX) and customer experience (CX) are intrinsically linked. I strongly believe that your CX can't outperform your EX for any prolonged period of time. Your culture has to be shaped to deliver your customer promises. This means that while it is possible to deliver service outcomes without too much concern about whether the culture is aligned, experience propositions can only be created and brought to life with the right culture. Customer experience is truly cultural.

Sometimes the distinctions are small. In our work in delivering an experience proposition with a nationwide holiday park company, I asked those in the front line, 'If you went on holiday to one of the other parks in the organization, how would you want to be treated?' The responses were tepid and uninspiring. We realized that their expectations were so low that as long as they were taken care of in the most basic ways, they would be really happy. So, we changed the question: 'If the most important person in your life went on holiday to one of the parks in the group, how would you want them to be treated and how would you want them to feel?' The question garnered a radically different response. While there was much work still to be done, the genesis of their experience proposition was born.

Sometimes the experience distinctions come from significant decisions that you must make as a leadership team. One philosophical question that is useful to explore is whether you want to be Apple at its very best or Tesco at its very best.

Tesco led the UK supermarket sector in the 2000s into the 2010s based on a deep understanding of their customers' needs but also the experiences they wanted when shopping. Tesco's Clubcard data provided them with such detailed data that they could design each store with such precision that their customers felt that they were getting exactly want they wanted, where they wanted it, in their journey through the store. At its best the Tesco experience was built on a deep understanding of the customer needs.

Apple have revolutionized personal computing, mobile connections and communications, music and much more. Time and again, especially during their most iconic times, Apple would create products and experiences that we as their customers didn't even know that we wanted. Obvious examples include the iPod that we didn't know we needed when we were reasonably happy with our MP3 players. We didn't know we wanted or needed a device that does the incalculable number of things that an iPhone does. We didn't know that we needed small devices that we can attach to things or people to track them on our phones.

But if we set aside the incredible products, there are other elements of the Apple experience that they created, that, if we had been surveyed, we would never have suggested. The whole Apple store experience was revolutionary, from the layout to the genius bar, to the education sessions. Even the packaging and experience of opening an Apple product was fundamentally different, and, vitally, it was different from what any customer would have asked for.

So, back to the question, does your organization want to be Apple at its best or Tesco at its best? Do you want to create an experience that your customer would never even dream of, or do you want to create experiences that meet every whim and need your customers could have. There is not a single right answer, but having these conversations in your organization is at the heart of developing your experience proposition.

Unique and distinct experiences

Many of the clients that I work with have world-class products. Indeed, I have worked with some of the most iconic customer experiences and attractions in the world, from the London Eye, to Ski Dubai, from Warner Bros Studios' The Making of Harry Potter to the world's most extensive collection of Tudor artefacts at the Mary Rose Trust, and many more.

While each of these attractions is wonderful and their product is truly amazing, their competition is too. Let's take Ski Dubai as one example. Ski Dubai is an indoor ski resort in the middle of one of the biggest shopping malls in the world. Despite the consistent heat of Dubai, Ski Dubai's temperatures are consistently maintained at −1 degree to 2 degrees Celsius throughout the year to keep the real snow at a perfect consistency for skiing down its 400 metre run on its 85 metre mountain. The resort features boxes, rails and kickers that are changed on a regular basis. It has a quad lift and a tow lift as well as a ski school for beginners. It is a truly amazing product that in many locations could corner the market. However, a short metro journey away is the tallest building in the world, with breathtaking views from its observation level. Next to that is one of the world's largest aquariums with the single largest tank in the world which holds ten million litres of water. A thirty-minute car ride away is Legoland Dubai Resort which sits on a footprint with three other theme parks, while fifteen minutes in the other direction is the world's largest and tallest observation wheel – the Ain Dubai – which stands 274 metres tall.

This is not an advert for Dubai's tourist attractions, but an illustration of why it is so important for the team at Ski Dubai to focus as much on the experience their people create for their guests and visitors as on the product itself. It is the customer experience that will ultimately define where the visitors choose to spend their dirhams when they visit Dubai, or certainly where their loyalties lie the second time they visit.

This is why the CX that you define for your organization must distinguish you from your competition. In some cases you could create a customer experience proposition that you believe is unique, but in many cases it will be the small distinguishing factors that set you apart and increase the sense of loyalty that you customers, guests, visitors and clients have towards you and, perhaps more importantly, increase the share of their wallet that they are psychologically ready to allocate to you.

Three drivers of loyalty

The pursuit of customer loyalty follows a well-worn path for many of my clients, but you may work in an organization that is just getting to a scale where loyalty comes through more than having a great relationship with an individual, or you may be in an organization that up to now has relied on the belief that a good product is enough. For those of you exploring loyalty for the first time, you are likely to be met by a barrage of information and research suggesting that a specific expert's view of loyalty is the only way. I believe it is much more useful to view loyalty in a more multifaceted way. Instead of one route to loyalty, I see three. While any one of these might be right for you, it is advantageous to explore whether a focus on a combination of two or more of them may help shape the distinct experience that you want your customers to have.

Loyalty driver 1: Experience moments

I would subtitle this as 'Small things, done brilliantly, every time'. You know those moments where the waiter in a restaurant just does a really great job throughout a meal. Or a call centre agent holds a great conversation with you, answers all of your questions and leaves you feeling happier and more optimistic than you were before your call.

Over the years I have spent as much time in the hotels at the Alton Towers Resort as in any other hotels. They are brilliant at experience moments. I would often walk the whole length of the two hotels that adjoin each other, from Splash Landings' reception through to the Spa at Alton Towers Hotel. Without fail, every member of staff would smile and greet me. This includes any maintenance staff or house-keeping staff who, in other hotels, would not necessarily see 'customer service' as part of their job. Small things, done brilliantly, every time undoubtedly drives loyalty.

These experience moments can be created online too, through clarity and simplicity. Digital creators could do well to pay close attention to this in my experience as the customer journey is often inconsistent. This is fine if I don't have a choice but to use your service or product, but if I can choose to take my custom elsewhere, viewing the user journey through the lens of how we can bring positive consistency to each small step the user has to take will have a big impact on loyalty.

Loyalty driver 2: Ease

If you are in the service industry and haven't already explored the customer ease revolution, then now is the time. Customer ease (or the reduction in customer effort) can, according to some research, increase loyalty by up to 88 per cent. How easy is it for your customer to buy from you? How much effort is required to get help? How easy is it to check in to your hotel or access your online support?

If you work in an organization that includes a contact centre, this really could be your experience distinction. While I appreciate that many contact centres are driving their customers to service their accounts or address their issues online, ease of connection and re-solution for those who do want or need to get through is a big win.

From my formative days in contact centres, I'm confident that if you work in a call centre, first call resolution will be a measure for you. And in many cases, this is calculated by the adviser asking some version of 'Have I solved this for you?' When the customer says yes, it's a big tick, job done. However, the challenge is that often the customers don't know if their issue really is resolved. Especially when it comes to technical issues, we find ourselves doing what the adviser has told us, only to discover it didn't actually work. So we call back and you wonder why, despite brilliant first call resolution stats, your advisers are still taking repeat calls from the same customers.

This played out recently for me. I called my mobile phone provider to arrange a handset upgrade. I waited over twenty minutes to get through, which wasn't a great experience. When I did connect with an adviser, he was great and took me through the upgrade process perfectly. The call ended with him asking if there was anything else he could help with, I answered 'No', and completed the NPS (net promoter score) questionnaire that was sent through following the call, giving top ratings for every category. However, the following day the new phone arrived along with a new bill. Unfortunately, the bill was nearly twenty pounds a month more than I expected. Of course, I called back. Despite being a first call resolution stat, I was back in the queue – for fifteen minutes this time – relating to the same upgrade.

The issue was solved easily in this instance, but it illustrates why a much more accurate measure of the experience the customer is having, and of the resources the organization needs, is 'calls per event'. This will enable the organization to review which challenges led to repeat calls and, therefore, how the processes and procedures need to be tweaked to avoid these repeat calls. The real challenge with first call resolution is that customers often think their issue has been resolved but have to call back due to a downstream issue. These aren't captured in traditional 'first call resolution' stats. First call resolution is a service measure, calls per event is an experience measure.

Loyalty driver 3: Wow moments

At first glance, wow moments can appear to be the most obvious of the loyalty principles. There are so many opportunities to wow your guests, customers, visitors or clients, but as you weave wows into your culture, two things must be kept in mind. One is that wows can cost money and the wow for the guest has to be worth the payoff. The second is that a wow can set a new bar of expectation for them. If it's a wow that is significant and costs the organization, the customer should get a sense that it is a rare occurrence. If you have ever received a free upgrade on an airline, then you know what I mean. I had flown long haul for years before my first upgrade. Yet, on every long-haul flight since I have waited for the call from the gate staff to give me the nod to head for the comfier seats. And there is a sense of disappointment with the airline when I don't get the call.

Wow moments don't always require huge investment but will return any investment made if presented in the right way. Whether it is the unprompted replacement of a dropped ice-cream, the unrequested upgrade of a hire car or hotel room for a regular customer, or an occasional invitation into the VIP queue in a theme park, all are what my good friend and advocate of brilliant customer experiences, Michael Heppell, would call 'wee wows'. These are small moments that made a big difference and are sure to increase loyalty, advocacy and future wallet share.

One of the most interesting things we have discovered in our work in this field is how few businesses capture and share stories of wow moments that their customers and guests have. We believe that diffusing wow stories throughout your business sets a precedent for others to do the same.

These drivers of loyalty aren't necessarily complex but are exponentially more difficult without the support of an ALIGNED® culture.

Here are three steps you can take to bring more of these loyalty principles to life in your organization.

1 Each loyalty principle increases the likelihood of another being played out. Review which are already happening in your

organization, encourage more of them, and focus on how the others can be dialled up.

2 If you are senior enough, re-examine your customer strategy. Make the loyalty principles focal in that strategy.

3 If you can't influence the strategy then look for marginal gains. Simple things done well can make a huge difference, but even marginal gains must be measured.

Measuring guest experience

This isn't a chapter on the intricacies of measuring customer experience. It is important, though, to consider how you will align your measures with every other part of your ALIGNED® approach.

Your measures have to show when and how you are delivering experiences that add strategic value. Your measures must also capture clearly whether you are living your experience principles, and I would argue that any measures beyond this are superfluous. You will, I am sure, have experienced those customer service surveys that are so cumbersome that they in themselves detract from the experience that you had. Avoid this at all costs.

We worked with a client who built their whole experience proposition around three specific experience principles. The research behind these principles was robust enough for them to have absolute certainty that if their guests experienced those principles, it would drive loyalty, wallet share and return visitation. They also had the technology and processes for them to continue to measure whether this was the case.

All of these combined meant that their key customer feedback was captured from four questions. Three were scaled questions, asking the degree to which the guest resonated with each of the experience principles. The fourth was the traditional NPS question. And while there were optional free text fields accompanying each question, and a final invite to contribute more detailed feedback, the process was valuable to the organization while still being simple and straightforward for the guest.

A word on NPS

Net promoter score is a metric that helps businesses gauge the quality of their customer service, particularly in relation to their competitors. If you haven't studied NPS before, it was developed from a body of work by Fred Reichheld and a team from the consultancy Bain and Company, in the early 2000s. The team launched a research project to determine whether a radically simple approach could provide the ultimate question to predict loyalty and the lifetime value of a customer. They worked with data supplied by the customer data analytics company Satmetrix, and tested a variety of questions to see how well the answers correlated with customer behaviour.

Their findings suggested one question provided the clearest predictor of behaviour:

How likely are you to recommend company X to a friend or colleague?

High scores on this question are suggested to correlate strongly with repurchases, referrals and other customer behaviours that contribute to a company's growth. Traditionally the NPS question is accompanied by a scale from 0 to 100. However, over recent years, an increasing number of organizations are moving to a 0 to 10 scale. The scores are calculated by subtracting the detracting scores (0–60 or 0–6 depending on the scale) from the promoting scores (90–100 or 9–10 depending on the scale) to give an NPS score.

In a recent piece of research by the US organization Retently, NPS scores by industry ranged from 4 on a 0 to 100 scale for the internet software and sales industry to 71 for the insurance industry. In 2022 Amazon's NPS score was reported to be 63, while Apple's was an impressive 72.

Net promoter score has spread to become the single most popular customer survey metric worldwide, and this is without doubt part of its value. It is the best and simplest way to compare the experience that your guests, customers, visitors and clients are having against the guests, customers, visitors and clients of your competitors.

NPS does, though, have its critics and potential limitations. In the context of your specific customer experience proposition, I would recommend some constructive dialogue between you and your senior colleagues as to whether it really gives you the data that you need, or whether you use it simply because lots of other organizations use it.

In the interests of balance to the wide fanfare around NPS, here are some of its criticisms. Some are technical, around the construction of the survey. Some are more specific about the data that it does or doesn't provide:

- NPS is built on an eleven-point Likert scale. It is broadly accepted that five or seven-point Likert scales are much more valuable in terms of their predictive validity. In other words, an eleven-point scale is too broad.

- The fact that those people who score 6 (or 60) or below are classed as detractors is an arbitrary cut-off. Reichheld is commonly quoted as confirming this. There is no evidence to support that if you give a score of 6 (or 60) or less that you will actually be openly critical of the organization or service you received.

- Finally, and most importantly, numerous pieces of research have suggested that a high NPS score is an unreliable predictor of loyalty, future spend, or share of wallet (the amount a consumer spends regularly on a product or service).

While I am an advocate of NPS as a solid comparative against how others in a particular industry are doing, and as a way to track whether our customers are generally happy with the experience they are having, my concern is that it is used too regularly as an indicator of growth or loyalty.

Let me give you two more examples of this. I regularly fly from Newcastle International Airport to London Heathrow Airport. It is a short-haul flight, and I find the whole experience more pleasant than going by train. So, when I get the 'would you recommend' question from British Airways, I generally answer as a promoter with a nine or ten on the NPS scale. However, that only tells part of the tale. It suggests I am loyal to British Airways. Yet the experiences I have with British Airways are generally poor. In fact, over the past five years or so, the experiences I have with them at most touch points, digitally, on the phone, in the airport and on the plane have continued to deteriorate. I am not loyal. If another airline started to fly from Newcastle to London, I would be sure to give it a go. My rating on the NPS scale in that case is based on a preference for flying over train travel. And on the monopoly that British Airways currently have on that route. It has little to do with how loyal I am as a customer, nor how good the experience is, nor on how likely I am to spend with them in the future.

The second example relates to the brilliant service experience that I had from the Volvo dealership on Scotswood Road in Newcastle upon Tyne. This was the dealership that we used when my wife had a Volvo and it required servicing. It was the single best experience that I have ever had when taking a car for a service. Everything was right. It felt personalized. There were small wow moments and it was brilliantly consistent at a high level. When the dealership rang to follow up on my visit, and to ask the NPS question, I gave it a strong 10 and told them how great they were. However, I have never been back to that dealership. We changed cars soon after and always have our cars serviced at the brand dealership of the car itself. So, for all I said I would recommend it, it was no predictor of my likelihood to spend there again. Add to this the fact that I would recommend them, but unless you happen to have a Volvo that requires servicing and you live somewhere close to Scotswood Road in Newcastle, my recommendation is likely to mean little to help the commercial outcomes of the brilliant team at Stoneacre Volvo Newcastle.

Outcomes are the foundation of ALIGNED® measurement

There are as many different ways to measure customer experience as there are ways to create it. Each will have their strengths and detractions, each will have their logistical and statistical positives and negatives. My strongest advocacy of all is that you design your experience measures purposefully and with your outcomes in mind.

If you believe the quickest way to growth and loyalty for your product is ease, ask your customers whether they found it easy to use and easier than your competitors.

If you are selling a luxury experience that you want your guests to tell others about, then ask them if they felt special and ask the NPS question. However, you may also want to follow up in three to six months to find out if they did actually recommend you and perhaps who they recommended you to.

If you have applied the ALIGNED® methodology throughout your organization, this outcomes-based measurement will be easier as you will be clearer on what your strategic and commercial outcomes are, but, broadly, my view on measures is the simpler and more concise the better, with one overriding caveat.

Your measures should be reviewable in as close to real time as possible and by every leader in the business.

If you are an experience business rather than a service business, then the experience that your customers, guests, visitors or clients are having today, matters today. Checking back and reviewing what happened a month ago is simply no good. Does this mean that I think the experience metrics should be obsessed over, every minute of every day? No, of course not, but having a community of people who are using the data to make decisions and interventions based on the most up-to-date information possible will give credibility and consistency to your experience proposition. The further away from this view-point you get, the weaker your proposition gets. Even if you are limited by the technology that you have in how 'real time' your data is, you have to find ways to collect and accurately collate your customer data as quickly as possible. You will reap the rewards. You will gain return on your investment in making this happen. The experience habits that you will grow by having the data now – or at least tomorrow – and using it immediately, will always outstrip the challenges of putting the processes in place to make it happen.

Let's not overlook for one moment that the data review and the interventions that are made as a result of these reviews are made by every leader. Or maybe more accurately, by any leader. I have made the point repeatedly through this book that experience is cultural. This means experience is how we 'be' in the organization. In turn, this means that our customer, guest, visitor or client experience is everyone's business. It is not solely the job of the head of customer experience to identify challenges and to put them right. Nor is it their job alone to give great feedback to those people at the frontline who are creating the environments within which those experiences can happen. Imagine being at the frontline of a business and getting a phone call from the IT director to say, 'Hey, well done, your guest experience scores yesterday were outstanding – you should be proud of yourself! Thank you.' Or a call from the chief financial officer to say, 'Hey, here's some feedback a guest has given. It's outstanding, so we thought you should know about it straight away.' It's a two-minute job, but it is the stuff of legends.

Even when things aren't going so well, knowing that your team are around you and are serious about helping to put things right shifts the dial in an experience organization. The moment someone like the chief people officer drops in on the chief customer officer and says, 'We can see a downward trend in the customers' measures in this area of the business. We know you've got it, but do you need us to do something?' is the moment that the organization really becomes experience focused.

Your experience measures do not have to be complex, but they do have to be outcomes focused. There are endless ways to measure experience. The most important thing is that you implement measures that give you the data that you need to create the experiences that you want for your customers. Don't simply go with the masses and implement measures because others use them. Most traditional call centres' metrics don't really give the data that is required, and even the most popular customer measure in the world, NPS, is an unreliable predictor of future behaviour. Use measures that work. Provide data in as close to real time as possible and make it everyone's job to review and intervene based on what the data is saying.

Here is one final experience story. It is one of my favourites and really underpins the difference between service and experience.

Many years ago, I coached Sophie Patrikios, Director of Customer Service for the Lego Group. Sophie is one of the most brilliant service leaders that I have come across in twenty years in the business. She kindly offered to give me a full tour of Lego's global contact centre at the time. One of the first things I noticed was that there were no prominent wall boards sharing information about call queues or call handling time or the other typical statistics that would be flashing away in a busy multilingual contract centre. This was unusual at the time.

On closer inspection I noticed that every agent's call set up, we used to call them turrets back in the day, had a small Tippex mark on it. I asked Sophie about this and she told me that underneath each Tippex mark was a light that flashed when there was a high volume of calls sat in that agent's particular call queue. She had gone round personally and Tippexed over this flashing light. This was baffling to me as, in pretty much every other call centre that I had worked in, this flashing light was notification to the call handler that they needed to get through their calls as efficiently as possible in order to help bring the call queue down.

Sophie told me that this was the opposite of what she wanted. The aim was for each adviser to get through a set number of calls per hour. This was not unusual in call centres. However, in Sophie's customer-experience-focused mind, it was as bad to get through the calls too quickly as it was to get through them too slowly. She told me quite emphatically that the call queues were not the adviser's issue. As the Director of Customer Service, it was her job to manage the resources to tackle whatever queues there may be. It was the adviser's job to love the one they were with.

In a busy world, where resources are tight and many organizations are driving more digital journeys and reducing live customer contact, insights like this are all the more important. The opportunity for what we used to call 'moments of truth' is, arguably, becoming more rare. It takes cultural insight and leadership savvy to ensure that your organization truly acts as an experience organization and to genuinely empower your people to live that culture.

The true meaning of brand

From a technical perspective, I am not a brand expert. Other than participating in the Mini MBA in Brand Management developed and led online by Professor Mark Ritson, I have no formal brand training. However, you need to have a clear definition and understanding of what brand really is. As I outlined in the definitions section earlier in the book, there is a misunderstanding that brand is the logo, the typeface and the visual representations of your organization. Increasingly, brand is also used as an interchangeable term for business – for example, by online 'entrepreneurs' who offer products to help you build a commercially successful brand. They mean a business. I always have reservations about handing over money to people who have such a fundamental misuse of terminology.

Brand is the feeling the customers and potential customers have about your business, your service and your products. In this definition you can probably see why we combined customer experience and brand, in its truest essence, into one factor. The X of the Alignment Advantage is experience plus brand. The two things are intrinsically interwoven. They aren't quite the same thing, but it is exceptionally difficult to separate them completely. Brand is measured differently to experience, but faces the same critique of the accuracy of well-known approaches to the measure of brand equity and value. In fact, the aforementioned Professor Mark Ritson held a live debate during which three world leaders in the field of brand equity and value were invited to state their case as to why their approach was the most reliable. The debate highlighted the wide disparity in the valuations the respective approaches designated to brand and their relative unreliability in predicting organizational performance.

That's not to say that I don't value brand, I really do. So much so that I think organizations, and those people in these organizations who are charged with shaping and managing their brand, should take a stronger strategic approach than is often the case. What I am philosophically at odds with is the short-termism and borderline virtue signalling that is often associated with, or justified by, the worst definitions of brand.

INTERVIEW Customer experience
Dan Rogoski

How often do you get to learn from a customer-centric leader who has facili-tated his attraction's rise to be the number one ranked visitor attraction in the United States, according to Tripadvisor? As well as his role as the Vice President of Operations for the Empire State Building Observatories, Dan Rogoski's career includes time at Madame Tussauds in New York and Washington and the day-to-day leadership of New York's The Ride throughout the Covid-19 pandemic.
   This interview is gold dust for any service leader.

What, for you, is the difference between customer service and customer experience?

I think this has evolved over the years. We have always had the term 'customer service' drummed into us, but really we are now in the experience world, and perhaps even more so in this post-Covid world. The distinction for me is that service is what you get as the customer from the attraction, or the hotel, or the place you visit. Experience is what the customer takes away from that visit or stay. The customer goes back home and what you aim to do is convert them into brand ambassadors for your attraction.

In our case we are trying to get our visitors to go home, tell their co-workers, tell their family, tell their friends, and tell their neighbours that they just had the greatest experience in New York City at the Empire State Building. When we do that, we are creating something important that really didn't cost you a dime. When we do this right we are creating ambassadors for the product and the whole experience.

As you know, I lead a lot of customer-focused training for our people, and during this summer's events I made a point about the amount of money we spend on getting customers into the funnel. People will know that the Empire State Building exists, but they may not know about the observatory portion of it, so they go online and they start to google Empire State Building. Then they get to our website. It's intriguing to them. They now get deeper into our website. They end up onto our calendar and decide to purchase a ticket or two. They end up in our cart (basket) and they buy because they have been convinced that this is going to be a great experience.

All those steps have been driven by a sales department and marketing department, a PR department, a social media department and lots more.

It's cost us millions of dollars a year in order to capture those customers and get them to trust us enough to put in their credit card details in order to get their e-tickets. It is up to us at that stage to create a world-class experience that matches the product that we are showcasing. We are proud to create that experience through five-star service, and if through doing that we have created just one brand ambassador that then goes home and talks to their family, friends and neighbours about just what a great experience it was, that costs us zero to get more people into the customer funnel. So that's really the message for us. We create that experience so that customers can go back home and tell others and that is great for them and great for us.

But it starts with the face-to-face customer experience. We rely on every one of our hosts within the observatory to do what they can to create the experience. We have a high level of expectation as to what we want them to deliver to each and every guest. And so if they deliver that and we get a positive result, you then have that customer experience that we strive for.

Thankfully over the course of the last few months we learned that we are the number one attraction in the country as rated by Tripadvisor. That position is based the number of reviews and then weighted against the number of five star reviews. We are number one in the country and number three in the world, and we are so very proud of that. What this award underlines for me is that we are getting the visitor experience right consistently.

To be the number one attraction in the United States and number three in the world is remarkable. You have an amazing attraction, there is no doubt about that, but there are other really good products our there among your competition. What have you done that has distinguished you from them, that's enabled you to become number one in the US?

I have been here for almost 11 months now and what just amazed me is the dedication of our customer-facing employees. At peak times we have more than 80 throughout the journey. They work varying schedules. We do a long day across seven days a week and there are a significant number of them that have been here a long time. Our longest-standing host has been at the Empire State Building for 38 years and it's just not something you see anywhere else. I was totally amazed because, typically, if you are host at an attraction, at a museum, at a theme park, if you are that customer-facing employee, you are here for a couple of years. Perhaps it's a job outside of college and you do it for a couple of years and then you transition into different roles. But I believe the authenticity of the Empire State Building, the history of the Empire State Building, the fact that we're in movies and TV shows and we are here in our 91st year in operation, I think that really sucks you in to what we're trying to accomplish here.

It is worth saying that we set our bar high. We are competing for dollars in the New York market. It is a busy market. There are lots of ways for our customers to spend their money so we don't just compare ourselves against other observation decks. We compare ourselves to everything. This includes bus tours, museums, boat tours, whatever there is in the New York attraction market we are comparing ourselves to and aiming to be better than. There is no attraction in the city that has the longevity and the dedication from their front-of-the-house staff that we do. That plays a major role in what we're able to accomplish here from a customer experience standpoint because it allows us to tell a story about, and behind, the attraction like nobody else can.

So, tell us more about how the story behind the attraction contributes to your visitors' experience.
We have video screens throughout the observatory and we call them 'host connections'. They are fully interactive so visitors can scroll through the screen and pick one of our existing hosts and learn more about their personal story. There are currently six hosts whose stories have been highlighted and that visitors can learn about. They get to find out about Tara's favourite restaurant in New York City and where Tara is from in New York City, as an example. This interactive mini experience is available in nine different languages and it really gives you the inside story of these hosts and why they've been at the Empire State Building for so long. This is a very distinctive connecting of the dots between our beautiful building and observation deck and those people who create the overall experience for the visitors. Of course, it also makes a very clear link between our culture as an organization and the visitor experience. It all emphasizes that the story of the Empire State Building draws people in, whether that is the people who work here or the visitors who join them on that journey on any particular day. It is a clear example of the employees' experience emanating out to the guest.

What would be your number one piece of advice for somebody who is aspiring to improve the experience that they create for their customers?
I have to share two. They may seem very simple, and may be obvious, but to me they really are the difference makers.

The first is that you have to treat everybody with respect. Respect is the foundation of high-performance teams. Without respect we can't build trust, and without trust there is no relationship between our people or our visitors and our attraction. Respect is demonstrated in simple but consistent ways. You have to acknowledge everybody. You have to know what their name is. If you can find out a little bit about their family then do that. You need talking points as you interact with everybody on a daily basis. I don't walk by anybody without saying hello. It may sound simple but for us those simple things have had a big impact within our business. I have been told that multiple people who previously held my position didn't necessarily have that same approach. I think they were surprised that when I arrived here 11 months ago that I made the effort to meet 100–120 people who were all still wearing facemasks due to the Covid-19 pandemic. Remembering 120 names and 120 faces wearing masks was daunting, especially when they only had to remember one new name, but I had to do it to show the respect I had for them and to acknowledge that everybody is playing a role and is a piece of the puzzle of delivering our objectives. So that is number one – *treat everybody with respect*.

My number two piece of advice is something that I have lived by for many years, because I was around leadership earlier in my career that didn't do this and I found it to be very frustrating – *never ask anybody to do anything that you wouldn't be prepared to do yourself*. That includes situations where I have to ask somebody to do something multiple times. I will jump in and do it myself because I think that shows and demonstrates that I am not just talking the talk, I am also walking the walk. I can go back to previous roles as well, whether that was at Merlin and jumping in the ball pit at Legoland Chicago because it needed to be cleaned and it hadn't been. I jumped in and cleaned it myself. When I was with The Ride, I found myself climbing underneath the bus and searching to try to find the source of an oil leak. It is very important to me to model the way and to not ask anybody to do anything that I would not do myself.

If there is one mistake that experience leaders must avoid, what is it?
Not calling out something that you see someone doing wrong. This is important, partly because it keeps everyone's standards high, and partly because that is a teachable moment for everybody. For example, perhaps you have walked through your museum or your attraction, and you have heard something that just didn't sound right in an interaction between your

host and a customer or visitor. Even if you just heard it quickly as you were walking by to do something else, it is very important later in the day to go back to that person and say, 'I just happened to be walking by, and I overheard how you said this. Perhaps you should have said it in a different way', or, 'Maybe if you said it this way the customer would have reacted differently.'

I think it is very important to take the opportunities to do this even on small things. I don't want them to think that I am micromanaging the process but I do want them to know that they are important enough to be on the end of a teachable moment. If as a result of that moment, they stop and think next time and maybe do things slightly different, then that has been a positive moment for everyone.

Among the myriad of important points Dan Rosogski touches upon, his final point underlines perfectly that customer experience is cultural. His assertion that experience leaders cannot avoid calling out when someone does something wrong is less about the specific impact in the moment on the customer or guest and more about setting the right standards culturally for that person and their colleagues.

10

ALIGNED® teams

Over the past two decades, I have worked with and observed some of the most amazing teams in the worlds of business and sport. If I were to make one observation above all others about what makes a great team a great team, it would be that great teams don't just happen. Standard teams come together with a brief to deliver what needs to be delivered, and the relationships and personalities within those teams are managed accordingly.

Great teams are those that are outstanding in the most literal meaning of the word. They are created with the end goals, both strategic and cultural, in mind. They work at being a team. They focus on relationships, not necessarily in a soft, let's all get along way, but to create an environment where every member of the team can instigate the conversations that need to happen to achieve what needs to be achieved.

In short, great teams are uncompromising about being great teams.

In this description, we already start to explore why the ALIGNED® approach helps these teams to create the Alignment Advantage. As referenced in previous chapters, the myth of 'starting with why', has become a staple in organizations. This is equally true in the teams that make up those organizations. Even in some early research we did as a team in TwentyOne Leadership, team purpose was suggested as the starting point for high performance teams. This focus on purpose misses an elementary, even earlier starting point. What is the strategic goal that the team exists to deliver? The starting point for a great team is strategic and commercial clarity. Without this, all attempts at team unity and high performance will fall short.

The team's strategic intent will heavily inform its shape and structure. This was highlighted again in a recent piece of research conducted for us by London School of Economics student Sakshi Mittal. She concluded that team structure provided the link between strategic intent and organizational culture. Your team must be structured to give it the best possible opportunity to deliver its strategic goals.

Only when these two steps are in place – strategic intent and the structure to deliver the strategic intent – can we really start to enable and embed the culture we need to deliver what we need to. To make the point clear again, your culture must be shaped so that it is a strategic enabler. If not, it will be a strategic blocker. This aligned understanding should give rise to some specific team-related questions. If you are the leader of the team, these questions cannot be avoided if you want to create an ALIGNED® team.

Is this a team or a work group?

When is a team not a team? This isn't set up to be a terrible joke. It is a genuine question. Not every team in an organization is actually a team. I am often asked to work with teams to help them be more collaborative and supportive of each other and break down silos. One of the first questions I always ask is, is it possible for one team member, or sub-team, to be successful while others are not? If the answer to this question is 'yes', then it is likely that this is a workgroup rather than a team.

For a team to be technically classed as a team, the individuals' goals have to be interdependent. One team member should not be able to fail completely, and every other team member be able to succeed. Without this interdependence, there will always be a degree of siloed operation.

Take a recent example from a 100 FTSE retail business. A senior director asked us to bring together her team, to align them and to break down silos within their regions. She wanted a strong, connected and consistently high-performing team. However, a quick examination of the organization's structure showed that each team member has their own lines of responsibility and their individual targets, against which each individual is very closely managed. While each member of the group has similar responsibilities, any interdependence is optional and relies on personal relationships between the group members.

No matter what relational work they did with the group, no matter how much their leader implored them to work closely together, there will always be silos, as that is how the organization is structured.

The redefinition of this group as a work group rather than a team in the traditional sense of the word is a vital step towards helping them to work in the most aligned way possible, not least because it raises a fundamental strategic and commercial question as to whether the organizational structure should be changed to make them a team.

So, the first step towards creating a genuinely ALIGNED® team is to define whether they are a team or a work group.

Can you afford to tolerate brilliant jerks?

Let me make clear that the answer to the question above is, almost definitely not! The circumstances where performance, experience or results should overshadow cultural mismatch are exceptionally rare. Brilliant jerks will, in most cases, ruin your team.

I also maintain that the management of individuals who deliver great results, or hold specific expertise, but are attitudinally wrong, is among the biggest and most difficult challenges for people leaders. The question that many of us ask ourselves in those cases is, can I afford to lose that person? The more powerful question, though, is, can I afford to keep them?

It may look on the surface like their experience is irreplaceable, but what if their attitude and behaviour is holding down those around them? What if their removal from the organization, or at least a correction in how they act towards their colleagues, would enable those around them to learn, grow and develop at a rapid rate?

You may feel that taking the person out of your team that delivers the best results is a risk to the overall performance of the team, but what if their attitude and behaviour is stunting the performance of others?

To be clear, brilliant jerks always hold their colleagues down. They always have a negative impact on the team that they are supposed to be part of. Unless you are convinced unequivocally that the others in the team would be negatively affected by their departure, you must take action to align their behaviours with the desired culture of the team. And if they aren't willing or able to do that, you must be ready to do what you can to move them on.

Does your team take joint and several responsibility?

Joint and several responsibility is a term that is most commonly associated with mortgages and lending. When two or more parties take out a secured loan, they are usually deemed to be jointly and severally responsible for the repayment of the loan. This means that each person is one hundred per cent responsible for the loan, and if the other party or parties default on paying the loan they must pay the full amount, as opposed to them being responsible for a percentage of the repayment.

Adopting this principle when it comes to a team's culture is a huge step towards creating a truly ALIGNED® team. Imagine, for a moment, that you join your colleagues for your monthly team meeting. During that meeting a number of actions are agreed, with each having an owner and a deadline. A month passes and then you join your colleagues again, with the first agenda item being the review of the previous month's actions. As each action is reviewed, it becomes clear that several of them have not been carried out because the individuals were busy, unclear on what they should have done or thought someone else would pick it up. What does this say about the culture of your team?

I am certain that you have witnessed this. You will have been part of teams where this was the norm. It may even be your team now. At best it is frustrating. At worst it impacts on the strategic and cultural performance of the organization. It mustn't be tolerated and the antidote is joint and several responsibility.

Let us run the scenario again, with a different philosophy in place. Imagine for a moment that you join your colleagues for your monthly team meeting. During that meeting a number of actions are agreed, with each having an owner and a deadline. At the midpoint between the last meeting and the next everyone reviews the actions from the meeting. You don't just review your own actions to ensure that you have done what you said you would do, but you also check to make sure that your colleagues have hit their deadlines too. You notice that one of the actions should have been completed and the result communicated, but you haven't heard anything. You pick up the phone to your colleague or drop them a message to check if they have done it or if they need any support. They thank you for the reminder and follow through on their action. In the next meeting the action review is quick and to the point as everyone has done what they said they would do. What does this say about the culture of the team? And what impact will this culture have on other teams and the performance of the organization?

Instilling a philosophy of joint and several responsibility means that it is everyone's job to ensure that we follow through on our promises. It stops unnecessary and unproductive finger-pointing and drives performance and delivery. It doesn't, however, diminish accountability. Suppose I have committed to something and don't deliver, especially when my colleagues have prompted me. In that case, it is very clear where the accountability lies and my colleagues and my boss can act accordingly.

Joint and several accountability isn't just for meetings – it should be embedded as a philosophy into every area of a team's operation and will drive performance across strategy, culture and the external experience.

What is most important – a high-performance team or a high-performing team?

This is a delicate and under explored distinction but is, in many ways, the link between the previous two points. It is especially important to consider if you are the leader of the team. The key distinction is whether as a leader you are most interested in the process or the outcome.

I am going to use a football analogy to explore this point. For over fifteen years, I have trained elite professional football managers in the UK to be even better leaders and to develop cultures in their clubs and within their squads that will help them get better results. The process-versus-outcome debate is one that, in many cases, produces a desirable and real answer in the minds of those participating in it.

Football managers and coaches regularly say that it is all about the process. If we follow the right process, the outcome will take care of itself. This means that if the team trains in the right way, is fit enough and implements the technical and tactical plans then the results will come. They will say that they don't need to focus on the result, they need to focus on the process.

However, these very same managers and head coaches know that the average tenure of someone in their position in the UK is somewhere just below twelve months. Football in the UK is a results-driven industry and a run of losses will very quickly lead to their dismissal. When this is the culture that they are in, how can they not be obsessed by results? This leads to short-term thinking and decision-making. It leads them to bring people into their teams and groups that may not be the best cultural fit but they know that individual's performances could quite literally keep them in a job.

This process – outcome distinction – isn't just relevant in football. In organizations there are times when we just have to deliver the results at all costs. Remember, in ALIGNED® thinking, culture is created to deliver the results that we want and need. If you need to create a high-performing team that delivers the outcomes at the short-term detriment of the balance in the team, then that is a decision you must make as a leader.

In most cases I urge you to create a team that is high-performance. High-performance teams focus on their processes. They trust that by getting their individual and collective performances right, the outcomes will follow.

When the pressure is on, pause and reflect – do you need to create a high-performing team or a high-performance team?

Do you trust each other enough to have the right degree of conflict?

Make no mistake, trust and conflict go hand-in-hand. You can't have a healthy amount of one without a healthy amount of the other, and together they form a strong foundation for the alignment and performance of your team.

At the heart of so many conversations about team development and leadership lies the question of how to develop trust and, while the topic is a complex one, the reality for you if you are a leader is that you must go first. We can rationalize that trust must be earned, but that isn't the foundation upon which healthy, long-lasting relationships are really built.

When individuals feel trusted, they are most likely to step into that sense of trust and live up to the expectation that has been set. We can develop that sense of trust by being honest about the things that we are good at and the things that we aren't. As leaders, we must follow through on our promises and consistently do what we say we are going to do. We must demonstrate through our actions and decisions that the things that we say are important actually are. We don't have to get things right one hundred per cent of the time. In fact, those occasions when we don't get things right are great opportunities to build trust. The vulnerability to admit when you're wrong, provides fuel for the flame of trust.

Being the living embodiment of trust will without doubt plant the seeds for trust to grow between the constituents of your team, but you must do more to nurture and nourish it. You must create opportunities for people to get to know each other. While not everyone has to bare their souls around the campfire, there is no doubt that trust grows through human connection. You must create clear boundaries of accountability, to avoid the sense that constituents are stepping on each other's toes as this erodes trust, even when it is inadvertent. Finally, your team members must know, unequivocally, that they must follow through on their promises to each other. If we remember that the fundamental definition of trust is a 'firm belief in the reliability, truth, or ability of someone or something', then we must be unrelenting in the delivery of our promises to each other. Without this as a core principle of how we operate in our team, we can never have the strongest bond of trust possible.

As trust grows, we can have more of the right kind of conflict in the team. Having been around teams in a coaching, leading or advisory role for twenty years, one thing is for sure about conflict. People are scared of it. Those on the outside of commercial organizations think that they are really robust, challenging environments, but most aren't. In most organizations, and in their constituent team, any modicum of conflict is swept under the carpet. It is squashed, hidden, ignored for fear that it will get in the way of the job getting done.

Ironically, the opposite is true. A lack of the right kind of conflict is one of the main contributors to under-productivity in organizations and the chances are you have been part of this at some point in your career. We have all sat in meetings where decisions are apparently made. Yet, despite the collective nodding of heads, most people in the meeting know that those decisions won't actually be followed through on because they don't really agree that they are the right thing to do in the first place. And why don't people voice their opinion in the moment? Because of a discomfort with conflict. And why does that sense of discomfort linger long enough and strong enough to prevent us from speaking up? Because of a lack of trust in our fellow team members.

Let's flip this around. When we do have the right degree of trust, we participant in those meetings and when a decision is being made that we don't think is right, we do one of two things. The first is that we challenge, with care and respect, the decision that is made. We tell people that we believe that this is the wrong thing to do. We tell them what we think we should do instead and we tell them why, and we do it in the belief that they will see the good intention behind our challenge. We also know, although it might not even occur to us at the time, that our challenge will not be seen as a personal attack, nor will it be held against us in the future.

The second thing that can happen, is a sign of deep trust. It is what Patrick Lencioni the renowned team development expert, calls 'disagree and commit'. When we truly trust our colleagues and they are taking a decision you disagree with, but one that comes from their expertise, then we are more willing to air our disagreement and commitment in the same sentence. When we have the trust in our colleagues to say 'This is not what I would do, but I know you are the one who is accountable for it, so I will completely support your decision', the game changes for performance and culture within our team. If you are the leader of the team, you must take any opportunity to model this and you should make it your mission to promote and recognize this show of trust and conflict when it happens.

Gaining the Alignment Advantage within a team is in many ways a microcosm of doing so within an organization as a whole. Everything that I focused on throughout this book applies; however, I acknowledge that there may be some broader strategic, cultural and customer and brand challenges that sit outside of our sphere of influence. By following the core philosophy of being uncompromising about being a great team and implementing the principles and practices from this chapter, you will build a high-performance and ultimately high-performing team, regardless of what others in your organization are doing.

INTERVIEW Brand and branding
Ross Aitken

Ross Aitken is the Director and founder of several branding-related organizations including The Product Room. He has worked in a consulting and advisory role for clients including Virgin Money, the NHS, Newcastle United, Samsung UK and Tesco Bank.

He was a huge influence in the development of the ALIGNED® methodology and on shaping the Alignment Advantage. He has one of the most practical and effective views on brand and branding that I have experienced, and takes a unique approach that unlocks the potential of his clients' brand and makes them look even better than they did before.

This interview gives a flavour of his distinctive perspective on brand and branding.

What is your definition of brand?

Often it is easier to talk about what isn't brand. Brand isn't just a logo. Brand isn't just a website. Brand isn't the communications that you put out.

A simple definition is that your brand is your reputation. Your reputation is all the activities your business carries out, including strategic work, the operational work, what you sell, how you sell it and every product you create, multiplied by how the client, customer, visitor or guest feels about what you do. That's what I think brand is.

If you agree with that, you have to accept the uncomfortable reality that, ultimately, your brand is not in your control. It is one of the reasons that brand experts inside and outside of organizations focus so much on logos, typography and colour pallets so they feel like they are in control of the brand. But really, brand is about how others feel, which means you can influence brand, but you don't own or control it. Different people have different emotions and reactions, and the art and science of brand is to do what needs to be done to ensure that you create the reputation that you want to, in as many of the people as you want to.

This means that the starting point of any brand conversation must always be, how do you want the customer to feel? And then you work back from there. This shouldn't be a unilateral decision. It has to be based on proper research and analytics. Unfortunately, too many organizations dive into the codifying of their brand before really understanding what it should be.

How does brand help to attract customers when the organization doesn't entirely control it?

Another way to describe brand is a business organization with a personality. We've all got a personality, and different people are drawn to different personalities for different reasons. If you start from the point of view of shaping your business' personality to attract customers who share that personality or want to be connected with it, you will be much more purposeful in your brand-related activities. You have to ensure that you're creating a brand that your customers or clients are attracted to, rather than one to which those who lead the business are drawn. Every week, I see brand managers inadvertently making the mistake of creating a brand they would be attracted to when they aren't the target audience for the service or product.

Can you give an example of organizations that have created well-aligned brands?

Let us compare and contrast Apple with Sports Direct. Apple stores are part of the Apple experience. The environment has a personality that is attractive to a certain consumer. How their people act reflects the personality. Even the fact that they have Geniuses rather than assistants or even specialists is an influencing factor. When you go into an Apple store, you expect everything about it to be a certain way and aligned with the product. And it is all at a price.

Similarly, if you go into Sports Direct, which has built its brand on a different pricing model, we don't expect a great experience within a store. However, we do expect to be able to get all of the products we want at the lowest possible price, and everything about the experience is reflective of that. Both propositions are attractive to their chosen customer bases. Where organizations begin to falter is where their personality isn't clear, or is confusing. When that happens, people stop feeling the way you want them to about the things that you do.

So there is a case for shaping a brand deliberately so it isn't attractive to certain customers, clients, visitors or guests?

Anyone who is familiar with Seth Gordon's work will probably be familiar with the idea of creating the smallest viable market. Your strategy should tell you how much you need to grow, what profit you need to make, or what you need to deliver to succeed. It will drive not only the culture but how the business needs to operate, how large or small, and how lean or luxurious it will be. These things will, in turn, influence how exclusive your brand will be. We associate the word exclusive with quality or price, but the whole point of making a product or service exclusive is that it excludes some people, which in turn makes it exceptionally appealing, compelling and desirable to others. Clearly, if you want a brand to be exclusive, certain influencing principles must be at play, including price, environment and behaviour. They have to be shaped to attract certain personalities and exclude others. I wouldn't be comfortable walking into a boutique fashion house, but that is because I'm not the target market. If I am happily calling into your boutique fashion shop or hanging around on its website, your brand activities aren't aligned enough. Equally, their target market should love everything they do. They should feel like they are being waited on hand and foot and given a real premium experience. They should feel much more than just buying a handbag. That experience is really what that audience wants. The difference between a £50 handbag, a £500 handbag or a £5,000 handbag is the whole experience, not just the product. Too many organizations try to build an exclusive brand for the masses, which almost always fails.

Another example is the difference between the feeling people may get when they think of Dr Brown's baby products versus the Tommy Tippee brand. Everything from Dr Brown's has a kind of medical feeling that is very reassuring to many consumers. Tommy Tippee is a much warmer brand, helping the customers to enjoy the rollercoaster of being a parent. Both have great products and well-defined and curated brands.

While the Dr Brown's name is strong, as Michael Wolf would say, the name and logo are just stops on the brand journey. They are not the be-all and end-all, but are relevant. In a fast-moving consumer goods market, so is the packaging, the presentation and the dialogue around the product, and we can't ignore the product's performance. For something like a consultancy business, establishing a credible track record will have a more significant brand influence than the name. As will the behaviour and impact of the staff. All of these are small stops along the way to creating a brand, but all start with a clear understanding of who our customers are and how we want them to feel.

I want to go back to this point about logos. Anyone who has been around brand and branding for any length of time knows that the logo isn't the brand. We know that the starting point is to understand what we want our reputation to be, and the personality behind that, yet in so many instances, even with big clients, the rebrand starts and ends with a new logo and website. Why is that?
Deciding to change the logo is a big decision for many companies, and I think that's to do with a sense of control. If those in charge of the brand feel like they are losing control of their reputation, or want to change how people feel about the business or product, the logo is a tangible change, even though the impact is likely to be minimal.

Of course, how long the product or business has been around, and depending on how much history and meaning the logo has, it may be a significant piece of the puzzle, but it still is just one piece.

One of the big parcel firms has just changed its branding, including its logo and name. I can completely see why they would do that, as their reputation for care and consistency is not good. If the business is not doing so well, it can feel like an easy fix to change the name to change the reputation, but if they don't fix the process and structures causing the reputational issues, the time and money they spend on the new name and logo will be wasted. If the parcel is three days late or left in unsafe places, it doesn't matter what they're called or what the logo looks like.

Let's go back to brand being your reputation, and your reputation being what you do multiplied by how your customers feel. That particular organization may reflect in the future that the significant amount of money they have invested in their rebrand would have been better spent on staff training or more vans or electric vans.

What is the biggest mistake you see people and organizations making regarding brand?

Not asking the right questions at the beginning of the process or asking them and not answering them. We have already talked about establishing what we want the brand experience to be. Nailing that down at the beginning of the process is vital.

Another question that we push our clients hard to answer is, are we solving the right problem here? I am a designer at heart, so I know how easy it is to get into the look and feel of branding. Colour palettes, logos, names and fonts are all stops on the journey, but they are not the destination. The destination is communicating what you want your personality to be to the people you want it to be communicated to. The destination is enhancing your reputation or getting your clients, guests, visitors or customers to feel the way you want them to feel about you. Without answering the hard questions, understanding the problems we are looking to solve, without creating the right strategies to create and deliver what we want to create and deliver, we risk spending a load of money on the latest fad.

The smartest brand people do their thinking before their spending. One of the most impressive things about Ross Aitken is his ability to simplify the complex. In so many organizations of all sizes there are misconceptions, misunderstandings and misalignment around brand. In the same way that the leaders in your organization must have aligned understandings of what the customer experience you are aiming to create is, then a shared understanding of brand is equally important.

11

ALIGNED® communication

Show me an organization that communicates well, and I will show you an organization that performs well. Show me an organization in which its constituents feel like they get the information and messages that they want and need, and I will show you an organization that has a strong culture. Show me an organization that conveys its key messages effectively to its key customers and I will show you an organization that creates brilliant brand and customer experiences. Communication is at the heart of the ALIGNED® approach and is crucial to grabbing the Alignment Advantage. When a client asks us to help them, their teams and their organization to be better at communicating, I always remind them that communication is pretty much everything in the business world. It is such a broad topic that many millions of books and many billions of words have been dedicated to the subject. Yet I am still going to be bold enough to suggest that there is a simple ALIGNED® framework that can help you be even better at communicating, regardless of how many of those books you have already read. Indeed, I would go so far as to say that if you have people throughout your organization who use this approach to design their key communications, it will revolutionize the impact that you all have. It will make messages stick, reduce the amount of communication that misses the mark and virtually eradicate worthless messaging. Intrigued? Then read on, but be warned, this approach, like all the others in the book, only works if you use it.

Outcome-driven

I cannot make the point strongly enough that I believe that the number one opportunity to make communication better in most organizations and indeed in more relationships of all types, is to make it more outcome-focused. All communication should have an outcome. Every email that we send, we do so with the aim of getting someone to do something differently. Everything has a reason, an impact, an outcome. If you ever have the urge to send information 'just for information' then don't. If you don't want the recipient to do anything different as a result of reading it, it isn't worth sharing. If you do want them to do something differently, and that might include a feeling, then be more precise about your outcome before you shape the message.

Before you communicate in any form, be crystal clear on what the outcome of the communication is before you do anything else. There are hundreds of occasions where I have picked up the phone to call a colleague or client and put it back down again while I consider what the purpose of the call is. What do I actually want them to do, think or feel as a result of this conversation? When I write a proposal or paper for a client, even though I have done this thousands of times before, I always start by capturing my specific outcomes for writing the paper before I commit a single letter to the page. Every meeting that I lead has an outcome.

As an aside, in a world where so many leaders spend so much time in meetings, the biggest shift in the meeting culture will come from a greater degree of outcome clarity. Why are we having the meeting? What will we do as a result? If the outcome starts with 'to discuss', that is not a meeting worth having or attending. Those discussions must result in an action, an agreement, a plan, an outcome. This clarity of meeting outcome will also impact who should and shouldn't attend the meeting. If you can't get that clarity (and if it won't be career limiting), don't attend. If it is your meeting and you don't have an outcome, then don't hold it until you do.

Aligned communication of all types – digital or face-to-face, individual or large-scale – must always start with an outcome.

State-driven

If outcome-driven communication is rare, then state-driven communication is so exceptionally uncommon that it is hard to give many examples of it happening in the day-to-day communications of organizations. Yet, when I share the principle and process with participants on the leadership programmes that I lead, it appears so obvious that they can't believe they aren't doing it all the time.

If the first question in ALIGNED® communication is 'What is the outcome?' then the second always is, 'What state do I need the receiver to be in, in order it make it more likely that the outcome is achieved?' More simply the question could be, 'How do I need them to feel in order to do what I want them to do?' Some outcomes may require a sense of excitement. Others may need a feeling of inclusion. Some outcomes might require a sense of unease. There are as many states as there are outcomes.

Here is an example of communication that was outcome-driven and state-driven from a piece of work I was involved in with a large energy company some years ago. After a number of unfortunate work-based accidents, this pan-European organization placed a huge emphasis on creating a culture of zero tolerance when it came to health and safety risks and challenges. In fact, to their credit, zero harm became their number one strategic imperative. The internal communications team produced wave after wave of zero harm focused communications, from team briefings to cascade packs. The executive teams embarked on tours of their respective countries to underline and underpin the messages. Yet, despite the concerted efforts and the consistency of information, the impact was negligible. If we were to examine the communications and assume the outcome, we would probably come up with the answer that zero harm is really important to the company and some of the jobs you do are dangerous. For many it felt like Captain Obvious addressing his troops.

When I was invited into the conversation, I suggested that the outcome of the whole zero harm initiative was actually to ensure that every child who had a parent, grandparent or guardian working for the organization got them back home safe and well at the end of every day. As I shared my simple thought with the senior team, the atmosphere in the room changed palpably. Together we went on to explore what states would be most likely to help us to achieve that outcome. We found that they would vary in different areas of the organization. For those hardy people working on the frontline who had heard the same safety briefings day-in, day-out for years and in some cases decades, we needed to engage them with a slight sense of 'Oh sh*t' in order to generate just the right amount of cortisol to keep them safe and ensure they got home to their kids and grandkids. For those people responsible for creating the new approaches to engaging others in the business in the initiative, we had to reinvigorate and stoke their excitement. For the leadership team we had to help them maintain their sense of focus, which by this point was already being challenged as the number one strategic imperative by some rather worrying commercial numbers.

With this clarity about the outcome and the states that needed to be generated to meet that outcome, the organization could now confidently move to the third and final stage of the ALIGNED® communication framework.

Experience-driven

Unless you are already using the ALIGNED® approach to communication, the likelihood is that the starting point for most of your communication is the content. You will, with really good intention, launch straight into the facts and figures or the research behind the proposal you are just about to make. It is this thinking that drives us to rely too heavily on supports like PowerPoint.

If you follow the ALIGNED® approach to communication, the content becomes the last stage of the process. Having asked, 'What is the outcome?' then, 'What state do I need them to be in, in order to best achieve that outcome?' the final question is, 'What experience do I need to create, to best generate the state and meet the outcome?' That's not to say that the experience couldn't be a presentation, but it's unlikely to be the traditional pore-and-snore type of PowerPoint that many people fall back upon. We have to remember that pretty much anything that anyone needs to know in an organization is written down somewhere. It's in a procedure's manual or on an intranet. It is in a book or stuck on a wall. The best approach is rarely to hose people with information; instead we must create an experience that gives enough information and gives people the right incentive for them to find out the rest for themselves.

In the previous zero harm scenario, frontline engineers moved from having a safety brief every day to creating risk scenarios for others in their team, who had to spot the risk and relate the resolution of that risk to specific safety procedures. This generated a sense of 'Oh sh*t' for each other, because there was a shared understanding that if one of them could imagine the scenario, then it could happen if they didn't all have their eyes on the ball.

Even in our written proposals to new clients, we create a structure and focus points to help generate a sense of excitement about working with us, to move that client a step closer to saying yes to us being their partner and to raise a slight feeling of concern about working with anyone else. In many cases we construct the paper around four questions that teacher and learning innovator Bernice McCarthy identified as being on the minds of most audiences. They are:

1 Why? Why this, why you, why should I pay attention?

2 What? What is the proposition, what is different about your organization?

3 How? How will we work together? What are the practicalities of the partnership or project?

4 What if? What if this goes brilliantly well? What are the other possibilities? What if it doesn't go well? What are the risks?

Even in a formal written paper, following the ALIGNED® framework, being outcome-driven, state-driven and experience-driven and then shaping that experience by using McCarthy's questions, we can create a very different impact than taking a more traditional approach. In fact, our conversation rate is staggeringly high by the time we get to the proposal stage, with well over 90 per cent of proposals we submit achieving the outcome of getting a 'yes' from the client.

In whatever format and for whichever audience, taking the ALIGNED® approach to communication will increase the impact and success of your communication immeasurably. It is important, too, that this simple framework can help enormously in grasping the Alignment Advantage for your communication. One of the consistent themes we see in engagement surveys is that even when a good, solid strategy is in place, people feel that it hasn't been communicated well. Using the outcome, state and experience (OSE) communication approach when planning strategic communication will ensure that you hit the right notes and get the message across to your people. Equally, once your culture is embedded, it is vital to keep the cultural message strong and consistent. The ALIGNED® communication framework will ensure that conversations about culture will remain engaging and valuable for people at all levels of your organization. Finally, brand and customer experience communications are ideal for the OSE framework to add value. Even the most experienced of marketers, brand experts or customer facing colleagues will be able to get their message across more concisely and effectively by using this approach.

Communication is all about outcomes, and when we clarify our outcomes and align the states that we want to create and the experiences that will help shape those outcomes then communication mastery will follow.

INTERVIEW Building the best consumer experience organizations
Jamie Charlesworth

Jamie Charlesworth has a remarkable record of leading visitor attractions across the world. Having started as a team leader in the newly opened water park in the Alton Towers hotel in the UK, he quickly progressed to become Operations Director of the historic Warwick Castle and to lead attractions and attraction clusters in Bahrain and Dubai, including the Dubai Aquarium in the heart of the famed Dubai Mall.

He is currently an Executive Director at Saudi Entertainment Ventures (SEVEN) who are building fifty cinemas, twenty entertainment complexes and at least two theme parks over the next seven years.

This interview highlights his insights drawn from leading people-facing teams and businesses across three different continents, on tiny budgets and with the most significant resources imaginable. The principles he shares and outlines are invaluable.

What are the key challenges for customer experience organizations right now?

I think too many experience organizations are looking at their toes. They are only looking at here and now, and it's not enough. I think a lot of people in experience organizations are referencing the Covid-19 pandemic as having slowed them down but there is a degree to which this is smoke and mirrors. There is a point at which we have to move on and say that the pandemic period can no longer be used as an excuse, and if we don't drive forward with customer-focused innovations then it is actually primarily because people are very comfortable with what they know and very comfortable with carrying on doing what was working for them before and is just about working for them today. Unfortunately, they then panic when things stop working and their business performance falls off a cliff. In many organizations that think they are customer-centric this is inevitable, because with a lot of these things they are fine until suddenly they are not. Occasionally the decline can be gradual, but what we have seen over the last few years is that people's opinions change very rapidly. We are in a world where social media has an almost instant influence and the amount of information you can access and absorb now means that customers' views can be swayed and change completely, very quickly.

What is the impact of this short-termism?

We will lose customers. We live in a world where our customers, guests and visitors have ever-increasing expectations. If we want customers to be loyal, recommend us and ultimately continue to spend their money with us, we have to look ahead. In most cases, continuing to do what we do now well won't be enough.

Here is a great example. Imagine you stay in a hotel and when you go to the room in the evening after your meal, the bed is turned down and there are slippers ready for you right next to the bed. Even if you don't use the slippers, you will think it is a nice touch. You will be impressed. Now my expectations from a hotel, and certainly that particular hotel, is that every night when you return to the room the bed will be turned down and the slippers will be out. This is the new minimum expectation and if it isn't done you will be disappointed. To compound this, if we are connected in social media and I mention the bed and the slippers, and you read it, that is now your expectation too. As customers, visitors and guests, we adapt our expectations a lot quicker than in the past and we know what we expect as the minimum. While I believe that social media is such a key factor in this process it isn't just social media. It is more the innately social environment in which we live that drives the increasing expectations.

As leaders of customer-centric organizations, the short-term view, where all we do is aim to recoup the losses of the last few years and react to the latest Tripadvisor review, will lead us down a potentially slippery slope. We live in a world were an Instagram post recommending a product or attraction can go viral and change the landscape for an organization, so we have to have the capability to influence the customer experience to make it more likely to happen, react to it when it happens but also to do our best to understand what experiences might cause that reaction in the next three to five years, not just today. That's why, at SEVEN, we build that emotional experience into the design of our attractions. We aren't just mapping what rides people can experience, we are designing around the experience we want them to have.

I know that this is all a balance in a world where the right people are at a premium but in the decision making mix has to be the fact that guest expectations are still increasing and some organizations are still promising that they can meet those expectations when in reality they cannot. Instead of innovating, or at worst being clear about their customer expectations, they cheapen their brand.

As a service profession, we have to be better at asking, how can we adapt? How can be more agile? How when we see this trend going in a certain direction, can we click our fingers and pivot that way? We can only do that by building our capability to look into the future and plan. If we don't, we will drive our customers away.

As service leaders, how do we build that ethos and capability?

As you know, this requires the right culture. As leaders, we must ingrain service-based principles and practices throughout the organization. Customer or guest experience has to be a focal part of our strategy. If not, we aren't actually taking it seriously. The experience ethos has to be alive in our vision and values. The senior leadership community has to do more than be involved – they have to believe in it and demonstrate they believe in it. Only through that kind of serious commitment does the ethos filter down into how we recruit and who we recruit.

When we hire the right people who have the right experience ethos, or can develop and we develop them properly and we look after them with the right benefits, and we measure their performance fairly and in a motivational way, then everything shifts. That ability to look ahead and pivot becomes more natural. Ideally, and not many organizations achieve this, it isn't just the end customer experience that pivots, but the organization's culture becomes organic enough that it can flex with what's happening around it.

Leadership in organizations like ours is about creating the conditions in which all of these pieces actually start fitting together nicely. It is not about one individual thing – it is all of these things and more. We have to make sure we are delivering what we need to today, but the real job is to develop a truly forward-thinking mentality.

What separates the really great ones in terms of best guest experience and customer experience versus the rest?
The single most important thing is the people that they hire. Average service organizations hire people that they think can do the job. Really good experience organizations hire people that are ready and willing to be developed and led to create the experiences that we want our customers and guests to have. But the thing that defines the really great experience organizations, I believe, is that they employ the right people to embellish their experience proposition and the culture behind it. They find people who will push the boundaries positively. These people have less of a need to be led. They naturally go in that direction. They may need some nurturing and some guidance, but they don't need to be managed in the traditional way. The more that any organization focuses on finding these people, and rewarding them and keeping them, then experience all becomes deeply cultural.

It is worth remembering that in this enormously connected and social world that we live in, we want our customers and guests to connect with others and recommend our attractions. Yet, how many organizations put the same degree of focus on ensuring that our people have an experience that they want to share with others inside and outside of the organization? How many organizations pay attention to the degree that their best people are ready to recommend the organization to other potential colleagues?

When you are looking for people who you think can drive the culture and the experience, what kinds of things are you looking for?

One of the key things I look for is intrigue. I am always compelled by candidates who ask questions. I'm not talking about answering the question with a question, or those who have prepared questions, but those who I feel really want to know more about the organization or the vision or our guests. I am always less likely to hire someone who feels like they are saying what they think they should or just giving good answers and I'm more likely to hire those that lead you into an interesting conversation. This is easier than it might sound, as you cannot fake fascination. You see a natural reaction of interest, and when I get that I very quickly think, right, that is the person we want. Even if they don't have all of the technical skills to do the job, even if they don't have all of the right qualifications, I know that is the profile and person that we should be hiring.

If we are looking for people who are passionate and have the emotional connection to create experiences then we cannot hire them through robotic recruitment processes. This philosophy should be carried through into the way that we develop people, too. When we train people who are already in the business, we what to engage and inspire them and we can't do that through traditional training approaches. And of course when we identify those successors who sit in our talent pools, we should look for that same degree of intrigue and value it at least as highly as technical expertise or experience.

I find it interesting that here in Saudi Arabia it feels like there is a higher proportion of natural leaders who do ask the questions. They seem to be intrinsically curious and want to know how they can do better, because leisure and entertainment and guest experience and all of the elements that create it are new to most people here. Many people haven't had the training yet. But they know what they want and what they don't want. And they know how they want to feel and they are able to articulate better than people in the UK and Europe often can, and all of this is a great foundation upon which we can build.

So, I want people who are intrigued and curious. I also want people who are able to make connections between what we want personally as customers, visitors and guests and how we can create those experiences for our organization's guests. That ability to connect, this helps hugely in our quest to shape our attractions and bring better experiences to life at every touch point. Because our people want to be developed and they have high expectations, all we are doing is helping them manifest experiences for others that have high expectations. We are giving them a stage to do what they already know how to do.

This itself becomes cyclical. Our people are feeding in their own suggestions on how we should shape experiences and I love this positive pushback. Its like they are giving me the information and the tools to create something that has never been created before in this part of the world. The openness to new ideas and new approaches has been remarkable and I think that is a broad cultural thing with the people we work with, and is also something that we have harnessed, nurtured and developed.

What you seem to be pointing to, again, is the importance of culture on the external guest experience. So just how important do you believe it is to have the right culture in an organization to enable the creation of the right guest experience?
I think it is an absolute staple and cannot be forgotten about, ever. But there has to be a pivot between culture and guest experience, as they consistently influence each other. While we are shaping the culture we have to understand who we are serving, what we are delivering and what we are looking to create. For example, all companies I have been involved with previously from the UK, or even in the UAE, are established; that cultural element has already been settled and they have got data because they have had guests coming through for five or ten years, or in some cases for decades. And because the brand promise and the whole external experience is established, I think that affects how people see and live the culture.

And here in Saudi Arabia that process hasn't really started yet. So, while the development of our organizational culture has to be a key pillar, which we get, we also accept that it will be refined as we start mass operations. The culture will shape the guests' experiences but the guests' experience will refine the culture over time.

All of the work in developing the culture, brand and guest experience is in support of a crystal clear strategic intent.
Absolutely. We have a very clear strategic direction. It is probably one of the clearest directions in any company I've worked with. Everyone here knows where we're going. We have to support the delivery of the strategic objectives as laid out in the Kingdom's 2030 vision. We know what we have to do for the country and also for our company. It's very unusual to have that

degree of clarity and while it is hugely ambitious and challenging, it doesn't feel complex. That clarity allows us to shape how we will deliver that in terms of operational plans but also the culture that we need to create. We are going to open twenty complexes and two theme parks. We are going to have 142 attractions. That kind of strategic intent requires a certain culture to deliver it.

The cultural narrative that we develop will mirror the ambition and lack of complexity that the strategic narrative has. And in turn that will help us to create better guest experiences than anyone else. This won't just be achieved because our people will be brilliantly trained, or because our facilities are going to be beautifully designed or because our car parking is going to be amazingly intuitive. The experiences will be powered by a culture that is lived and breathed by all of our people and will exude in every interaction.

Acknowledging that many of your guests will not have been to a theme park before, how do you set about shaping amazing experiences for people who really don't know what to expect?
As with anything customer-focused, we started with solid research. Our initial market research included interviews with over 25,000 people, to actually understand which of the various concepts we have will land best. That was just one of the steps. That research isn't a one-off. It is an ongoing part of our business plan. Every year we go back out to the regions, not just the main cities like Riyad or Jeddah, but the secondary cities as well, and touch base with them because this country is changing and developing at a rapid rate. We will continue to do these temperature checks and make sure we continue on the right path. We want to set a new bar in guest experience and that means pushing the boundaries, but we must do this in a respectful way. Our face-to-face interactions will have to have a degree of personalization to them; the standardized Disney-type approach just won't work here and what will be right in Jeddah is unlikely to be right in Al Hasa. The ongoing research will play a key role in ensuring that what we do is based on a solid understanding of what we can do and where we can innovate best on those understandings.

We will keep this research going way beyond our main openings. We will continue to want to know, are we still on track? The data coming into us from live operations will ensure that our experiences will set the new standards for guest experiences in the Kingdom and beyond. Customer analytics aren't of course unique to our organization, but I'm a huge believer in taking the customer research and organization's vision of what the experience should be and merging them together to create something special.

My ambition is to create the new standard that everyone else aspires to reach. From the moment the guests start to interact with us to the end of their journey, way after they leave our attraction, they will feel the SEVEN experience. This ambition won't be achieved with a load of data and one day of training when people join us. It starts with a cultural ambition that will be shared from our management team all the way through the organization.

I know that it will require good leadership throughout the organization. We are going to have to embed ourselves, understand our teams and stay in touch with what they are delivering, and make sure that everyone continues to understand why we create experiences and how everyone contributes. All these things together will keep the standards unreasonably high.

You have said a lot about the importance of customer data – what about data on your people?
That is the piece of data that is often overlooked. Of course it is important that we focus on the guest research, but are we analytical about our guest experience enablers? We research the right food and beverage for guests, but do we fuel up the people who serve that food properly? Do we create the right environment behind the scenes?

Over the years, I have seen customer organizations give their new people a warm and fuzzy feeling inside when they start. Their people know where they are going and what they should be doing. They have had a great onboarding experience. And then suddenly they discover that they don't actually have the right tools to do their job. If we are going to create experiences that set a new bar, we must know immediately if our people are feeling like this. We have to collect data about our team's happiness, engagement and connection with their colleagues. And we have to act on that data. We can't be a typical organization that does annual staff surveys and takes six months to do anything with the information.

If we want to be agile for our guests, this requires agility with and for our people. This is another point where hard data and visceral experience must connect. We could collect masses of data and have it analysed by the greatest data scientists but if we haven't created an environment, a culture where people feel like they can tell the truth about the experience they are having with the organization and what could be better, then the data and its outputs are meaningless.

If you were to give one piece of advice to a new customer experience leader, what would it be?
I would say that 'simple' is probably the most underrated word in the whole guest journey. It is so easy to over-complicate things, and all the stakeholders, the leaders, the management companies, the training companies want to show the value that they can add. All of these things add layers to the process and create complexity. New experience leaders should consistently ask, 'How do we keep this simple?' I know that in the past I have been guilty of changing things completely when what I should have done is simplified them.

Complexity is cyclical. We can invest lots of money to changing something which didn't need wholesale changes, which means we need to keep refreshing to justify the investment. Then we invest in measuring to prove the value of the original investment. I'm not saying this is never right, but the starting point for new leaders should be, how do we keep this simple? Ask how we turn paragraphs into sentences. Literally and metaphorically.

You have worked in organizations that create brilliant experiences with huge budgets and tiny budgets, and this principle seems to apply in both.
You are absolutely right, because great guest or customer experiences don't cost money. There may be an investment of time, especially in listening to the voice of the guest and listening to the market around you but even that doesn't have to cost a lot of money.

What and how you implement the experience proposition is defined by the size of the organization and the budget, but the individual interactions don't cost money. In larger organizations with bigger budgets you can invest more in support systems but you have to recoup that value. In smaller organizations with smaller budgets the focus should be on creating those moments that make a difference at every touch point. And in as simple a way as possible. My experience is that in smaller organizations it is easier to connect emotionally to the customer.

As the organization or the budget gets bigger, we put pillars in place to maintain that sense of connection, but they should be kept simple. The real investment tends to come when we want to market what we do to a broader audience, but we mustn't confuse marketing with customer experience. They aren't the same thing. And whether we market to ten people or ten million people and whether we lead ten people or ten million people, as leaders we must maintain and convey our passion for what we are trying to achieve.

Maybe they are the two principles for experience leaders of organizations of any size, simplicity and passion. If we get them right, lots of the rest of what we need will follow.

Jamie Charlesworth covers a lot of ground in this interview. His vast experience from the smallest of organizations to the largest and from the tightest of budgets to the most extensive highlights that the principles of customer and guest experience remain the same. While tighter budgets and resources require a greater degree of creativity, larger budgets and resources demand more impressive results. Either way, all focus must be on aligning everything that we can to create the experience we want our customers to have.

12

Living an aligned life

On a recent episode of the business podcast *The Diary of a CEO*, entrepreneur, investor and star of *Dragon's Den* Steven Bartlett pointed to health as the tectonic plate upon which all other areas of life sit. He followed this up in a recent tweet, saying, 'If the pandemic has taught me anything, it's that we have nothing without our health – our health is our first foundation. Our dreams, ambitions, experiences, relationships and passions are all contingent on a foundation of good health – without our health, we have nothing.'

I couldn't agree more. Indeed, I believe that as a leader, you should make it a strategic imperative that you and the rest of your team are prioritizing their physical and mental health.

The pandemic really has been life-changing in so many ways. The primary alteration I see in many of the leaders I work with is that life has become much busier. Almost everyone I work with worldwide is 'always on'. There is no balance and no alignment. People are doing more than ever. We are all trying to fit so much in, yet many of us are feeling a sense of dissatisfaction that we aren't quite doing well enough at anything. For many of us it is time to live a more aligned life. This was never intended to be a personal development book. In fact, this chapter wasn't in the original proposal I created, but I believe for many – including myself – it could be the most important of all. To paraphrase Steven Bartlett, without alignment we have nothing.

Your life strategy

One of the greatest drivers of a sense of discomfort in life is the feeling that we are working really hard, yet achieving nothing. I experience it from the wealthiest people that I coach. They have all of these material things, yet still feel a deep sense of want. It is a sure-fire sign that their goals are misaligned.

It is OK for us to want to achieve things. I think that in the last decades drive for purpose, the attainment of other things, like material goods, wealth and physical health has been somewhat tarnished. Yet, we all know that goal-setting is good, so why not set targets that excite and inspire us, regardless if they are materialistic? I would rather be in the pursuit of a materialistic goal that lights me up so much that I wouldn't not try to achieve it, than set some well-meaning goals that I don't have energy for.

In the interview that closes this chapter, the extraordinary coach Paul Mort shares his goal-setting approach, which is an outstanding structure to follow. I would add to it the need, at the beginning of the process, to ask yourself repeatedly, 'What do I really want?'

Here is how this played out for one of my goals at the beginning of the year. I starting writing a goal about health and fitness. I wanted to be fitter. I asked myself, 'What do I really want?' That honed it down to: I want to look better, slimmer, more toned. Again, I challenged this with 'What do I really want?' I don't want to just look better. I want to be healthier. The process continued until the goal emerged, 'By the end of the year, I want to be measurably stronger and healthier, and feel happier with the reflection of my body I see in the mirror.' I knew this was right as it excited me when I read it. It also pointed to some pretty specific enablers. For example, I had never lifted a weight in my life before this year. My goal told me that was something that I needed to do. I couldn't be stronger without knowing how strong I am and then improving on it.

I'm sure that you have noticed that the goal is SMART, or at least smart-ish. I love a life vision; I will come on to that soon. However, the pursuit of an aligned life requires some degree of goal-setting rigour to set us on the right path.

Of course, health goals aren't the only ones worth setting. Most people also have a selection of goals related to finance, relationships and social life, career, family, personal development and contribution. Don't feel tied to any specific combination. The priority again is to set goals that you will delight in the pursuit of. Once those goals are set, you can use the same strategic process as you would for your business to create sub-goals and eventually actions to bring those goals to life.

How do you want your life to be?

Remember my favourite definition of culture? Culture is how we want to 'be' around here. Well, how do you want your life to be over the next year? Do you want it to be as busy as it has been over the last couple of years? Do you want it to be busier, richer, more fulfilling? How do you want to feel, how do you want to behave? What will you demonstrate is important by the habits you follow and the decisions you make?

So much misalignment in life comes from a lack of fulfilment. Specific, conscious focus on creating the culture we want for ourselves is such a great way to achieve fulfilment. By aligning our personal purpose, values and vision, we are explicitly creating the life we want to lead.

As with organizational culture, we don't have to create a narrative that includes all three of purpose, values and vision. I do worry sometimes that people get so tied up in finding their purpose, that they miss the opportunity to achieve wonderful things. I certainly think that the discovery of personal values, and the alignment of our actions with them, is a vital step in creating the personal Alignment Advantage. Here are some fundamental questions to answer when exploring how you want your life to be:

Purpose:

- Why do you do what you do?
- What makes you grateful?

- What mark do you want your life to leave?
- What would you do if it didn't matter whether you achieved it or not?
- If you didn't have to do anything in particular, what would you do?
- How do you want to contribute to the world?
- If God existed, what would you want him to say to you as you enter the pearly gates?

Values:

- What values are the most important to you? (Look to identify between four and eight.)
- If these are your values, which are you living most aligned to?
- Which requires new habits to ensure that you are living your values?
- Who in your life shares most of your values?

Vision:

- If you were to fast-forward eighteen months to three years into the future and your life was the most wonderful you can possibly imagine, what are all of the ways that you would know?
- How can you create the richest picture possible of this vision?
- What are the small steps you can take today to bring this vision closer to reality?

In answering just some of these questions, you are undoubtedly setting in place a life culture that will lead to alignment and joy.

Your life's X

Many of us feel the tensions in life between creating a great business and having great relationships. We all know that we should put our health first, but that implies we are putting our family second. We will always have a sense of misalignment unless we make the X – the external experiences we are creating – part of our life's plan.

The focus of our X will shift as we go through life. In my experience, as I have got older, my focus has moved from the importance of the experience I wanted to create for my parents and broad group of friends, to my colleagues and partner, to now my wife, children, close friends and clients. Whoever you are defining the X for, the same ALIGNED® principle applies – the culture that you create in your life will seep out into the experiences those around you have. If you feel stressed, they will feel it. If you are dissatisfied, they will feel it. If you are happy, joyful, healthy, they will feel those things too.

Here some questions to help you define the external experience that you want those around you to have of you:

- What do you want to model for those around you, including your children if you have them? How do you want to show up for your partner?

- How do you want to make those who you spend important time with feel?

- What do you want people to say about you when you aren't in the room?

- What do you never want people saying about you?

- What experience do you want to create for your customers, colleagues, clients or workmates?

This definition of your X shouldn't be complex, indeed the more concise the better. However, it should excite you. It shouldn't feel like a negative pressure; rather, is should be another exciting goal to enjoy the pursuit of.

Align your life

When you have explored, reflected, designed and refined the three areas above, you must make sure that the goals and actions you have created align as per the ALIGNED® methodology. Your life culture must support the achievement of the goals you want to achieve. Your life culture must also be a foundation from which you create the experiences that you want to create for the people around you.

Putting this framework into action, making it a cornerstone of how you shape your life, means that, perhaps for the first time in your life, you can have true balance between what you achieve, how you feel and how those around you experience you.

In doing this you will achieve and experience life's Alignment Advantage.

INTERVIEW Living an aligned and fulfilled life
Paul Mort

Paul Mort has twice been awarded UK Master Coach of the Year. He's a world-class coach and international speaker. He is a straight-talking, high-performing leader of businesspeople. He was formerly suicidal, overwhelmed and diagnosed bipolar. Mort stood on the edge of a cliff, ready to end it all, until his wife stood in front of him and asked him one pivotal question.

'Do you really want the kids to grow up as the kids whose Dad killed himself...?'

At that moment Paul knew he had to fight one last fight for his family, and set upon seeking out the world's foremost experts. And since then, his books, courses, videos and content have reached the lives of millions of people. Now Paul spends his time coaching people around the world to take control, find clarity, direction and inner peace while lighting a fire under them to chase their dreams and lead their family.

In this inspiring interview, he explains how we can all live the aligned, ful-filled lives that we all deserve.

What makes a goal useful or helpful when it comes to creating the life you want to lead?

First, let's be absolutely clear that setting the right goals is exceptionally important when it comes to an aligned life. If I don't have a goal or an out-come or a target, it's like driving around with no destination in mind. So every day I get up and have two choices – I'm going to be defined either by my past or by my vision of my future. We can try to be present, in the moment, but in reality my attention has to go somewhere. That is the path that most people are on. They are in a routine doing the same thing over and over again. For a lot of people, the hardest part of creating a change is just not doing what you did yesterday or the day before. That is why we need to be focused on the future. If I haven't created a goal, how can I put my attention on where I am going?

Not having a goal is like getting in a taxi and the taxi driver saying, 'Well, where you going?' And instead of saying where you want to go, you just say 'Not here.' It just doesn't work. My view is that we have to have something to move towards. I work with hundreds of people, many of them business owners. Lots of them have been successful before but they tell me they feel lost or stuck. These feelings absolutely go hand-in-hand with not knowing where you're going and not having a destination in mind. So, for me, goals give me somewhere to focus my attention.

Goals really create feelings of inspiration and excitement, and I think they are intoxicating feelings. In fact, I would go even further and say that the one common denominator in people that are suffering from any kind of depression is that they haven't created a compelling future. This is something that I have spoken to thousands of people about. The lack of a compelling vision of the future is a significant contributor to those feelings of depression and anxiety. I have spent lots of time reflecting on the suicidal thoughts I had. They came because I didn't have a compelling vision of the future. I felt that I had nothing to move towards and that I was going to go around in circles, and that was so incredibly tiring. I really believe that we must seek out challenge that inspires us. Life will always find a way to remind you that it's not about comfort. We need to set goals that inspire us, that compel us and excite us.

When I think about my goals, I want to feel electric. That happens when my goals feel slightly scary. If I think of things that I'm most proud of in my life, those that give me the most feelings of pride and gratitude, at some point I didn't know how I was going to achieve those. I think that sometimes people get so caught up in their thinking about how they will achieve their goals. And I would go further and say that I believe that the reason most people don't achieve their goals is because their goals are too boring. It's not because they're too hard, but they're too boring. They get stuck thinking about the 'how to', they lower their expectations and they get bored by them. When I set my target I am clear that I don't need to know at that stage how I'm going to achieve it. At that stage, the 'how to' is none of my business. I want to set goals that are so electrifying that I don't know how to do it, but I just know that I will.

Once we get to that stage, we start to work out who can help us to achieve what we want to achieve. That's one of my favourite questions. It comes from someone I have been working with since 2018 called Dan Sullivan. In 2020 Dan published his book *Who Not How*, and I'm obsessed with that question. Rather than getting caught in how we are going to do things, focus in on who can help me do this. It stops us from getting stuck. Who can open doors? Who's already doing it? Who already knows that person? When we have the vision of the future, the electrifying goal, then we can explore who can help us to move towards them.

Does that change when you are working with people, when you work with individuals who are really stuck? Does that goal just have to be scary and compelling for them, even though it may not be challenging for other people?
The real question, no matter what the starting point is, is if we were having this conversation six months from today, and you were looking back over the previous six months, what would have to have happened for you personally and professionally for you to be happy with your progress? This is a brilliant way to free up people's thinking about how big the goal is, and focus much more on making progress. It allows them to focus on action, on getting started, because sometimes the problem with big goals is that when people feel stuck, those goals seem so far away that people don't get started.

So, even with the most ambitious of visions, I don't believe that people should goal-set for more than three years in advance. I don't know about you, but I can't remember what I was doing five or ten years ago, so why would it be any different imagining out a goal five or ten years into the future? Three years is a great timeframe, because it is close enough that people can imagine what three years in the future can look like, but it is long enough to be able to chunk that three-year vision down. Eventually, those chunks will be so small and mechanical that it will become easy to move towards and achieve. A three-year vision is imaginative. It's creative. It's inspiring.

Next comes the process to make it achievable by being able to do a little bit every day. The next question is, 'How will I know that I'm a third of the way towards this three-year vision? In these answers I have my one-year goals. Now, 'How do I know that I am a quarter of the way towards those one-year goals?' Now I have my ninety-day goals. Suddenly I'm making that big vision small enough to progress towards. I'm making it bite-size. Next I ask, 'How will I know that I am a third of the way towards those ninety-day goals?' Now I have my thirty-day benchmarks. Finally, I ask, 'How will I know that I am a quarter of the way towards those thirty-day goals?' Now I've got things I can do this week. I have been able to make that vision so small that it's actionable every single day. Even if I am taking tiny steps. I am sure it's the same for you writing this book. Writing a book is a big job, a huge challenge, but pretty much anyone can write one word. The words turn into sentences and so on.

Even those people who are tremendously overwhelmed or stuck, with the right process, can find things that they can do to move them through this process to take them towards living an inspired life. To be clear, living an inspired or aligned life is about being able to take that ambitious three-year vision that lights me up inside and electrifies me and just make it so small that I can bring it into my attention daily and then take action towards it on a daily basis. In that way, it isn't about taking massive action, I just think it's about consistent, small actions.

How does the environment that the people you work with impact on their ability to live an inspired or aligned life?
There is a brilliant book by Benjamin Hardy in 2018, *Willpower Doesn't Work*, in which he talks about this concept of environment. Hardy says that if your environment is in opposition with your goals, all you are left with is will-power, and willpower has an expiry date. As a result of this insight, my whole environment, from my office here, to my classroom, to my podcast studio, to my bedroom, I aim to set them up so they are in line with my goals.

Your environment's critical. It is really challenging to outperform environment. I think you can rise above your environment every now and again, which is really important for people who are struggling or just getting going. It is important to temporarily become more than your environment, but without some changes you will eventually get dragged back into that environment. The truth and challenge for many people is that the most important thing in your environment is the people in it. There are times when you have to change the people that you spend most time with, I believe.

This is the very reason I take my kids to most of my events. They meet people who are exceptionally high performers in their respective fields. They have met the likes of Tyson Fury, Chris Ramsey, Gary Vaynerchuk and James Smith. These people are at the top of their fields, and to be in the same environment as these people can only, I believe, be good for my kids. This is partly because they realize that these people are just normal. They are normal people who work extraordinarily hard to make the most of their talents. And their environment is a vital part of that.

People sometimes refer to this as the law of conformity. We adjust our behaviour to conform to our peer group. Living an inspired or aligned life requires us to surround ourselves with people that we have to raise our bars to be around, rather than lower our standards and live a standard life.

I absolutely curate my environment, and would encourage everyone reading this to do the same, especially in respect of surrounding themselves with people who are heading in the same direction or have already achieved what they want to.

By the way, that doesn't mean that we never spend time with friends or family who aren't exactly where we are. I can catch up with old friends and enjoy their company for a little while. But I'm not going to conform to their standards. One example is that I haven't drunk alcohol in nine months. I have committed to not drinking alcohol for twelve months. I don't preach to my friends that they should do the same, but it also means that they know not to try and push me to have one. I am lucky that my friends don't, but if they tried to, I would separate myself from them even more.

Some people reading this would feel like not drinking alcohol would be a huge step. Why and how have you given up alcohol?
It is worth me saying that I didn't drink alcohol a lot anyway. During the whole lockdown period, I only drank twice, on two Fridays in a row. Generally, I might have drunk five or six times in a year, so maybe it wasn't as big a deal for me as it would be for others. Having said that, the timing was interesting.

In the time during Christmas and New Year I went to Dubai with my family. It is one of my favourite places. On the way back, we were on the flight home and I was doing the goal-setting practice that I mentioned earlier. As part of the process, I asked myself, what is going to stop me achieving these goals? I know I'm in a place right now where, mindset wise, I'm pretty on point. I'm able to manage my emotions as well as ever. I've got a brilliant network. I know how to do a lot of the work that I need to. There are some things that I'm still scared of, but really the two things that stop me the most are getting sick or getting injured. These are the two things that slow me down the most and drain the most energy. I realized that over the years the most common denominator with either of them was drinking alcohol. So, there and then, I made the commitment. On that flight, in that moment, I said to my wife, I'm not going to drink next year. Even she was surprised. She said, 'You hardly ever have a drink!' I just realized that I wanted to see what would happen and I made the commitment there and then. The benefits have been huge and I can't see a single downside.

During this nine months of not drinking, I had big insights. The first is that I only really drink when I already feel rubbish. This year I have had many opportunities to drink. I have been flown around the world as the VIP speaker at so many events. I have been to Portugal and Costa Rica, to name just two. I have filled theatres with my own live show in London and Newcastle. At no point have I really wanted to drink. I felt like, 'Why would I?' That's when I realized I have been feeling so good, I didn't want to drink. I only want to drink when I feel rubbish in the first place.

The other big insight comes from the number of times that people asked, 'Is it not boring?' I feel the opposite. I have set up this year in a way that drinking would be the most boring thing that I could do. Everything else is so electrifying that drinking, and therefore taking the edge off the rest of the stuff, would be insane. And I'm not spending my weeks doing exciting things and having boring weekends. I'm spending my weekends doing a lot of fun stuff. Alcohol would take the shine off all of that.

I am not saying that I am never going to drink again, or that people shouldn't drink at all, but I will say that it has been a great experience for me. My training has never been better. I am not getting sick anywhere near as much. I have been able to fit more in my schedule and get more done. My weekends are way more fun. I have created more magic moments. I have created a life which is so inspiring that I haven't got the time or the inclination to drink. That is amazing.

So, what is mindset?
Mindset, for me, is a set of beliefs and assumptions that we own that are so powerful that our behaviour conforms to them. We develop beliefs and assumptions that our behaviour falls in line with. That is mindset, to me.

We have to accept, then, that we can change our mindset, but in order to do that you have to challenge your assumptions and beliefs. This is something I continue to work on and to learn about. Once we reach the realization that 'I am in charge of how I feel and you are in charge of how you feel', things start to change quite quickly. That isn't to say that it is always easy, especially when we go through something traumatic like losing someone. Even in the most challenging of times, it is important to know that our mindset can help us through. A coach that I was working with during one of my most difficult times has this analogy about our lives being like the movies. We want lives like a blockbuster, not a boring thing. This means that there are going to be funny scenes, romantic scenes, death-defying scenes and heroes' journey scenes. But movies also have hard scenes. He asked me to work from the belief that we are only given out the scenes in the movie of our lives that we can handle.

Even in the most difficult times, I have been able to find an upside. It's not always easy but it is possible. That is mindset at its best. And it is important to say that I'm not trying to feel positive about it. I'm just looking to get balanced about it. I'm looking to get objective, because whenever I'm too positive I'm not seeing the downside, and whenever I'm too negative I'm not seeing the upside. So I'm out of balance. I always want to feel balanced – I want to see both sides.

I think balance is a great part of mindset. It is one of the reasons that my wife and I work so well together. She does all of the things that I don't like doing and vice versa. I love speaking in front of groups; she would hate to do that, but loves the process of organizing the gigs to make sure they run perfectly. When she first came into the business, some people could have felt like she was being negative, poking holes in things, but she brings objectivity and balance. She keeps my feet on the ground. Without her I would make crazy decisions. I would say yes to too many things. I would launch too many things. My wife is my balance. She keeps my decisions good and my feet on the ground, but she is also the person who helps me move from good to great.

When you see people trying to achieve an aligned and inspired life, what's the single biggest mistake they make?
Trying to change their output without changing their input. What I mean by that is that they're trying to change their actions, but they're not changing what's going on inside their mind. They want to perform better, or live better, but hand-in-hand with that has to be a change in what you read, what you watch, what you consume and how. And by consume, I mean what they listen to, eat, drink, sniff, everything. People try to change their outcomes

without first changing their habits. This links back to a point I made earlier. The mistake is allowing the environment to oppose the goals, then people wonder why they keep falling off their desired track. They go back to their defaults. They go back on autopilot. Their environment drags them back to their past, despite their goals.

When you have a methodology as powerful as ALIGNED®, why would you stop at applying it in business? In life as in work, we create a huge advantage when we stop and plan the connection between what we want from life, how we want the environment of life to be and what experiences we want to create for those around us. It is worth highlighting again that when we take care of ourselves, it allows us to show up at our best for our family, friends and colleagues.

I believe we are on the verge of a revolution. The impact and simplicity of the ALIGNED® approach is evident and I invite you, indeed urge you, to be in the next wave of leaders that grab the Alignment Advantage. Whether you are aligning your team or your whole organization, you have the opportunity to join the ever-growing band of people who are making a huge difference by connecting strategy, culture and customer experience.

INDEX

Aitken, R (brand expert) 16, 144
Aligned Advantage 63
ALIGNED® approach 12
ALIGNED® communication 145–59
    experience-driven 148–59
    interview 150–59 *see also* ALIGNED®
        communication: interview
    outcome-driven 146
    state-driven 147–48
ALIGNED® communication: interview
    – building the best customer
        experience organizations 150–59
    acknowledging many of your guests may
        not have been to a theme park
        before, how do you set about
        shaping amazing experiences for
        people who really don't know
        what to expect? 156–57
    advice for a new customer experience
        leader – what would it be? 158
    all of the work in developing the culture,
        brand and guest experience is in
        support of a crystal clear strategic
        intent 155–56
    as service leaders, how do we build that
        ethos and capability? 152–53
    if you were to give one piece of advice to
        a new customer experience leader,
        what would it be? 158
    what is the impact of this short-
        termism? 151–52
    what are the key challenges for customer
        experience organizations right
        now? 151
    what separates the really great ones in
        terms of best guest experience
        and customer experience versus
        the rest? 153
ALIGNED® methodolgy 5, 62, 109
    brilliant logic of 81
ALIGNED® performance management
        97–108 *see also* boxes *and*
        Bridgewater, S
    bringing ALIGNED® performance
        measurement together 100–108
    performance measures 97–100
        cultural mesures 99–100
        stretch measures 99

ALIGNED® teams 131–44
    can you afford to tolerate brilliant
        jerks? 133–34
    do you trust each other enough to have
        the right degree of conflict?
        137–39
    does your team take joint and several
        responsibility? 134–35
    interview: brand and branding *see*
        boxes
    is this a team or a work group? 132–33
    what is most important? – a high
        performance team or a high-
        performing team? 135–37
Apple 111, 112

Barrett, S 161
Becker, H 80
boxes (for)
    ALIGNED® communication *see*
        interview for ALIGNED®
        communication
    ALIGNED® teams: brand and
        branding -Ross Aitken 139–43
    can you give an example of
        organizations that have created
        well-aligned brands? 141
    how does brand help to attract
        customers when the organization
        doesn't entirely control it?
        140–41
    what is your definition of brands?
        140
    so there is a case for shaping a brand
        deliberately so it isn't attractive
        to certain customers, clients,
        visitors or guests? 141–42
    I want to go back to this point about
        logos 142–43
    what is the biggest mistake you see
        people and organizations making
        regarding brand? 143
crossing the cultural chasms: ensure
        the leadership team are fully
        committed and
aligned 79
interview: Culture: Emma Woods (and)
        65–71

any moments in your careers where culture
and brand felt at odds? 69
focusing on culture at what points in
your career? 66–68
how do you balance employee's needs
with those of customers? 69–70
NPS as your preferred customer measure:
do you have a preferred way
to measure teams and people? 70
was there any strategic or commercial
conflict in doing this? 69
what is your definition of culture? 66
your culture as a cornerstone for you/
your people 68
interview: living an aligned and fulfilled life:
Paul Mort 166–73
does that change when you work
with people, with stuck
individuals? 168–69
how does the environment impact on
the ability of people you work
with to live an inspired or aligned
life? 169–70
some reading this would feel that not
drinking alcohol would be a huge
step – why and how have you
given up alcohol? 170–71
so, what is mindset? 171–72
what makes a goal useful or helpful
when it comes to creating the life
you want to lead? 166–68
when you see people trying to achieve
an aligned and inspired life,
what's the single biggest mistake
they make? 173–74
interview: living an aligned and fulfilled
life 166–73
interview: what is the X and why –
customer experience: Dan
Rogoski 125–29
if there is one mistake that experience
leaders must avoid, what is it?
128
tell us more about how the story behind
the atrraction contributes to your
visitors' experience 127
what, for you, is the difference between
customer service and customer
experience? 125–26
what have you done that has
distinguished you from other
good products? 126–27
what would be your number one piece
of advice for someone aspiring

to improve the experience they
create for their customers?
127–28
Bridgewater, S 101–08 see also boxes
Bull, H (Divisional Director, Legoland
Windsor Resort) 18–19 see also
interviews
highlights impact of shifting the
three levers in ALIGNED®
methodology 16
busting business myths 5–12
myth 1: culture eats strategy for
breakfast 5–7
myth 2: great organizations start with
why 7–12

Charlesworth, J 150–59 see also interview
for ALIGNED® communication
Cialdini, Dr R 85, 86
crossing the cultural chasms (and)
73–96
the business case for cultural change
74–75
create a clear shared cultural narrative
78
create a strategy to bring the culture to
life 81
crossing the chasm 73–74
the curse of underestimating scale
78–79
define your cultural landing point (and)
75–78
example from a client 76–77
example from a sporting
environment 77
by three acid tests 76
develop and mobilize cross-level, cross-
discipline change teams
87–89
and areas for development 87–88
engaging the masses 81–82
ensure the leadership team are fully
committed and aligned (and)
79–81 see also Becker, H and
boxes
hedging and side-bet theory 79–81
getting to the cultural landing point (by)
93–95
1. make the new ways of working
your standard working practices
93–94
2. ensure all development or issues
underpin the new ways of
working 94

3. review the project and celebrate success 94–95
initiate multiple business projects with slightly unrealistic timescales 89–92
    and six questions for tackling policies, processes and procedures 91–92
the magic 20 per cent (and) 82–85
    how the magic 20 per cent creates scarcity 85–86
    how the magic 20 per cent creates social proof 86–87 see also Cidaldini, Dr
    the law of diffusion of innovation 83–85
        1. innovation 83–84
        2. early adopters 84
        3. early majority 84
        4. late majority 84
        5. laggards 84–85
    scarcity and social proof 85 see also Cialdini, Dr R
maintaining cultural consistency 95–96
customer data and its importance – what about data on your people? 157–58
when looking for people who can drive the culture and experience, what are you looking for? 154–55
what you seem to be pointing to, again, is the importance of culture on the external guest experience – just how important do you believe it is to have the right culture in an organisation to enable creation of the right guest experience? 155
you have said a lot about the importance of customer data – what about data on your people? 157–58
you have worked in organizations that create brilliant experiences with huge
budgets and tiny budgets, and this principle seems to apply to both 158–59

The Diary of a CEO podcast 161
Drucker, P 5, 40 (and) see also The Practice of Management
    management by objectives (MBO) concept (aka management by results (MBR) 40

Dubai 113
Durnford, T 44

Gander, J 45–47 see also interview strategy (box)

how to build an ALIGNED strategy (and/ by 49–58
    breaking down the key strategic objective into enabling objectives (and) 55–56
    a word on ownership 55
    continuing the strategic alignment process 56–57
    and Principle No 2 of building an ALIGNED® strategy: build it down, execute it up 56–57
    is your organization too fast-paced to have a proper strategy? 57–58
    and two fundamental questions to ask 58
    Principle number 1 development of strategy (and) 49–50
    challenges and revisiting the overall strategy 50–51
    stand-alone EOs (EO1–EO5) 50
    strategic alignment 53–54
    and two-day site visit (box) 53
    strategic fog (and) 51–53
    revisiting overall strategy to check for challenges 52–53
    scenario (box) 51–52
    variations of well-intended patchwork approach 52
how to gain the Alignment Advantage 27–38
    culture and the X 30
    culture is the pivot in the Alignment Advantage 30–38 see also interview for culture is the pivot in the Alignment Advantage
    highlights impact of shifting the three levers in the ALIGNED® methodology 16 Advantage 27–29
    six questions to start the Alignment Advantage 27–29
    and key points to note 28–29
    strategy and culture 29–30

iconic customer experiences and attractions 112
interview for culture is the pivot in the Alignment Advantage (and) 31–38

despite challenges, you were successful
in creating a cultural shift – how
did you achieve this? 35
how do you start making cultural
changes in a school environment?
32
how has adopting ALIGNED®
methodology helped in an
educational setting? 31–32
if a key factor in your application of
ALIGNED® methodology helped
to move the school from the
time you joined to where it was
when you left, what would it
be? 16–17
so while your strategy shaped your
culture and the cultured shaped
the external experience, as you
started to bring the external
experience to life, it supported
the embedding of the culture
and therefore the delivery of the
strategy 17–18
some reading this may feel this is very
hard work and a lot of time
was spent thinking instead of
doing 34
tell us more about how these cultural
shifts influenced the external
experiences you created 35–36
what are key challenges you hve faced
in shaping the culture to support
delivery of a school strategy? 35
what did the strategy look like in your
last school? What did that school
plan focus on primarily? 32–33
you mentioned Ofsted. To what degree
did the Ofsted framework
influence your strategy? 33–34
interview – ALIGNED® performance
management: strategy and
marketing: Sue
Bridgewater 101–08
creating a strategy – a complete piece of
work 102–03
how do you see an organization's culture
influencing the perception of its
customers? 107–08
how would you define strategy? 101–02
it seems that some organizations have a
gap between data they hold and
the marketing insight they gain
from it? 105

key insights and important learnings
of students, business leaders
and those in sporting
environments? 103–04
organizations best at marketing and
those not so good – what
separates the best from the
rest? 104
what would be the single most
important piece of marketing
research or insight that everyone
should know? 107
where does customer insight fit into all
of that? 106–07
where does brand fit into the whole
marketing experience? 105–06
you have worked with some of the best
marketers and some not so good
– what separates the best from
the rest? 104–05
your response when said the
organization moves too fast for a
strategy? 104
interviews:
living an aligned and fulfilled life
166–73 see also boxes
with Helen Bull, Divisional Director of
Legoland Windsor Resort 19–26
introduction – becoming part of the 5%
Club 1–4
how to make the most of this book 4
what is the 5% Club? 2–3

Jobs, S 7
Jones, D (CEO, Mary Rose Trust) 9–12 see
also interviews

key strategic objectives, more examples
of 43–45
the fast-growing multinational 43
the small but ambitious lifestyle business
(and) 43–45
elements important for business
success 43–44
phrase 'when we have' 44 see also
Durnford, T
what to avoid and KSO for a marketing
strategy 44–45
Kouzes, J 63

Law of Diffusion of Innovation (1962) 60
see also Rosen, E M
living an aligned life (and) 161–73

align your life 165–73 *see also* boxes
how do you want your life to be?
     163–64
    purpose 163–64
    values 164
    vision 164
    your life strategy 162–63
    your life's X 164–65
        and questions to define your external
            experience 165

McCarthy, B 149
Markkula, M 7
Meier, D 12
Mort, P 162, 166–73 *see also* boxes

Nelson, D 38

Posner, B 63
The Practice of Management 40 *see also*
        Drucker, P

references (for)
    busting business myths 12
    crossing the cultural chasms 96
    three key components of the ALIGNED
        framework 26
    truths and half-truths about culture 71
Rogiski, D 125–29 *see also* boxes
Rosen, E M 60 *see also* Law of Diffusion of
        Innovation (1962)

Sinek, S 7, 8, 12
SMART: specific, measurable, achievable,
        relevant, time-related 39–40,
        76
the strategic starting point (and) 39–48
    building a strategy (interview) 42
    chapter summary 45–48
        and interview strategy: Jonathan
            Gander 45–47
    defining your key strategies
        objective 40–42

interview strategy: Jonathan
        Gander 45–47
key strategic objectives, more examples
        of 42–45 *see also subject entry*

the three key components of the
        ALIGNED* framework
        (and) 13–26
culture 14–15
    definition of 14–15
    more terms to be aligned on 16–26 *see*
        also Bull, H
    client 17
    customer 17
    staff, people, colleagues or
        constituents 18
    talent 17–18
    visitor or guest 17
strategy 13–14
the X (and) 15–16
    brand 16
    customer experience 15–16
the truths and half-truths about culture
    59–71
    big bang launches don't work 60–61
    the brand values conflict 61
    creating a purpose, values and vision
        does not create a culture 60
    a good culture is a nice culture 61–62
    purpose and values – the
        distinctions 62–
        interview: culture: Emma Woods
        (box) 65–71 *see also* boxes
    purpose 62–63
    values 63–64
    values – language and number 65–
    71

what is the X and why? 109–29
    more on the service/experience
        distinction 110–
        and clarity of experience 110
Wozmak, S 7